THE RED BANDANNA

TOM RINALDI

PENGUIN PRESS | *New York* | 2016

PENGUIN PRESS
An imprint of Penguin Random House LLC
375 Hudson Street
New York, New York 10014
penguin.com

Photograph credits:
Pages 71, 111: Courtesy of Chuck Platz
137: U.S. Navy / Getty Images News
194: Jewel Samad / AFP / Getty Images
Other photographs courtesy of the Crowther Family

ISBN 9781594206771 (hardcover)
ISBN 9780698407480 (e-book)

Printed in the United States of America
1   3   5   7   9   10   8   6   4   2

Designed by Marysarah Quinn

FOR DIANNE, THE CERTAINTY.

FOR ALL, FOR WHOM THE DAY ENDURES.

"You can hold back from the suffering of the world.
You have free permission to do so and it is in accordance
with your nature. But perhaps this very holding back is
the one suffering you could have avoided."

—KAFKA

THEY WAITED AT BEDROCK.

Seven stories below the ground, seventy feet deep in the earth, they sat. On a bright spring morning, while flags flew at half-staff in the memorial plaza far above, some seven hundred had made the long descent to gather in this chamber. Together they met: strong and weak, mournful and hopeful, persistent and diminished. Families and firefighters, city officials and rescue workers, orphans and political leaders, they waited for the solemn ceremony to begin.

Shortly after ten-thirty A.M., the president of the United States stepped to the lectern, dressed in a black suit and tie. He faced a cavernous room called Foundation Hall, a soaring open space with remnants of twisted steel and an exposed sixty-four-foot-high slurry wall, bolted in place as if it were still holding back the tidal waters of the nearby Hudson River. The president looked out at the numbered seats and ordered rows set up for the program, at the day's invited guests, including the governors of New York and New Jersey, the previous two mayors of New York City and the one currently holding the office, and a former president and his wife, who was the current secretary of state.

In this hole in the heart of a city, in a quiet and somber voice, Barack Obama began his speech for the occasion: the dedication ceremony of the National September 11 Memorial Museum at ground zero.

If it were a time for platitudes or soaring themes, he chose not to use them. He spoke slowly, in the measured and deliberate cadence of an elegy. As he delivered his first words, a mother sat backstage. After the president's remarks were finished, she would walk to a different microphone and share some of her family's story. For now, she sat out of sight of the assembly. There was a television monitor set up for her to watch the president's address, but she couldn't bear to look. Her eyes remained on the floor.

In the second row of seats, directly behind the mayor of New York City, a father kept his chin up and eyes forward, looking toward the podium. It was good that his wife would soon speak for him and their family. He couldn't yet bear to; the emotion would overwhelm him. As the president spoke, he sat and listened. At the first mention of his son's name, he began to weep.

On September 11, 2001, in the worst terrorist attack in the history of America, 2,977 people died. Standing in the footprint of the fallen towers that spring morning, the president chose to speak about just one. He singled out a young man who helped save people he didn't know in the South Tower of the World Trade Center before its collapse. He recounted the scene in the 78th floor sky lobby. As fires burned and smoke filled the air, in darkness and chaos, a voice rose, leading people toward the stairs and then down seventeen flights to safety. One victim was too weak to make the descent, so he carried her across his back. When the young man reached a lower floor with clear air, he urged the group to continue down. Then he left them, turned around, and climbed those long flights back up, looking for others he might rescue. For months, the man's identity remained a mystery, but one clue had emerged, the common thread to the descriptions of the people he guided and carried.

"They didn't know his name," the president told those assembled at the ceremony. "They didn't know where he came from. But they knew their lives had been saved by the man in the red bandanna."

The words echoed across the hall and off a graffiti-covered steel beam, standing tall in this part of the museum, a remnant of the towers. Amid the colorful messages and notes scrawled across the steel of the I beam was a photo of the young man, a picture holding the promise that one day he would be found.

By the time he was recovered at ground zero in March 2002, six months after the towers collapsed, the truth was beginning to emerge. And so, too, would the story of his finest moments, his selfless, fatal choice on that September morning. Welles Crowther was the man in the red bandanna.

"All those who come here will have a chance to know the sacrifice of a young man," the president said toward the end of his speech. "A man who gave his life so others might live."

I

TAKE A MOMENT.

Take it out. Unfold it. Press your hand down upon it and flatten it, into the surface of your desk, or the edge of the bed, or along the line of your leg. Twenty-two inches along any side, four ounces in your hand, barely enough weight to notice. Polyester and cotton, dyed and printed, cut and packaged, folded and shipped, to reach you, one way or another, and land in your palm.

Pick it up. Look at it.

What do you see there, in the red, white, and black? Is there something in the ancient pattern and the Persian fig shape, the paisley teardrop and the flat pointed stars? A child's thing, a trifle, a rag?

What do you carry, what truth could it possibly contain? What meaning could it hold?

Fear and strength. Smoke and blood. Doubt and faith. Terror and valor. The dead and the maimed. The way out and the walk down. The sacrifice given, and the salvation granted. Living. Dying.

"It's all in there," the father says. "It's all in that bandanna."

They searched for the right name. He was their first, and they felt the weight of the decision. A name is the label for a life, the first thing you're given upon entering the world, and the heading for all you leave behind when you're gone.

Should they look to their lineage, to honor their bloodlines, or pick a name that would be free of the past, to accrue its own meaning over time?

In the end, history won, as it usually does. On May 17, 1977, in New York City, the first child of Alison and Jeff Crowther was born: Welles Remy Crowther.

The boy was named after a man his parents never met.

Henry Spalding Welles was Alison's great-uncle in several senses of the word, a figure shrouded in stories and tales, legends she'd heard about since childhood. A favorite of Alison's father, Frank, Uncle Henry led an outsized life, certainly by the family's telling. Despite living in Manhattan, he was an accomplished professional sportsman, working as a hired shot and public marksman, for Remington, America's oldest gun maker. As legend had it, Uncle Henry once hit two hundred clays in succession in competition, a display to prove the accuracy and effectiveness of Remington's newest shotgun. He also worked for True Temper, a manufacturer of fishing rods and reels, and was accomplished as a fly fisherman. Uncle Henry invented and held a patent for a diving plug, a wooden lure carved and weighted to penetrate the surface of the water, to help catch fish in any type of water, any time of day.

For Alison, it wasn't so much the tales as the way they were told, the spark that came into her father's voice when he spoke about Henry Spalding Welles, the look that crossed his face.

"I thought, what could be a better name?" Alison recalled. "There was just this magic about Uncle Henry." The stories about the man, the ones her family loved to tell with laughter and pride and wonder—about beating Annie Oakley in a shooting competition, about sailing wooden boats across the ponds of Central Park, about President Eisenhower using his trout fishing flies—all shared the theme of taking a bold and unpredicted line through life. It was a name they hoped their son would make his own.

Alison Remy's own line was a gentle loop, from the suburbs of Westchester to a campus in New England, then back south to Manhattan. She grew up in the house where her father did, the house her grandfather built on Shawnee Road in the wealthy village of Scarsdale, north of Manhattan. Her grandfather and father, Frank Remy Sr. and Frank Remy Jr., shared more than the family home; both were graduates of New York University, both were dentists, and both were athletes.

When Alison graduated from Scarsdale High School in 1966, she didn't follow the family path to NYU. Instead, she enrolled in Wheaton College in Norton, Massachusetts. Founded as a female seminary in 1834, Wheaton was one of the oldest colleges for women in America. There were antiwar protests during her time there, but the small school was far from an epicenter of the countercultural unrest exploding across American campuses in the late 1960s, and the academic environment was serious and challenging. The student body, twelve hundred women by the time Alison graduated, was expected to be diligent, studious, and involved. That worked for Alison, who was a dedicated student with a passion for environmental studies. She headed the first Earth Day celebration on campus.

The summer before her junior year, she went on a blind date set up by another couple. Alison got the call only after the woman originally scheduled for the date had to cancel and the matchmakers didn't want to stand the suitor up or hurt his feelings. When Jeff Crowther walked into the room, Alison had a completely novel reaction:

"It was love at first sight," she recalled. "It really was."

For Jeff Crowther, the fact that his first date had canceled, upsetting the night's original plans, fit his own line well enough. If there was a prescribed path, odds were he wasn't following it.

Jeff had grown up in White Plains, a larger, more diverse city just north of Scarsdale. His family had its roots in Maryland, but his father's work brought them to New York. Bosley Crowther, a *New York Times* reporter, writer, and critic, spent forty years with the paper. As a student at Princeton, he entered a current events contest cosponsored by the *Times* and a new weekly magazine called *Time*. His essay, on why the Calvin Coolidge administration should withdraw its forces in Nicaragua, won first place. The prize? A five-hundred-dollar check and a job offer with the *New York Times*.

Starting as a cub reporter in 1928, Crowther worked his way up to general reporter, rewrite man, feature writer, and then, in

1940, the paper's chief movie critic. He held the position for twenty-seven years, becoming an institution. Bosley's reviews held extraordinary weight, often setting up films for success or failure.

Though his father and grandfather had attended Princeton, Jeff went in a different direction. At his mother's suggestion, he headed to Clark University in Worcester, Massachusetts, a respected academic institution, though not overly challenging for him, at least not at first. He sailed through freshman year without developing any impulse to study, or even to attend classes regularly. By the end of his sophomore year, after spending his time betting on horses at a local track, playing pool in the basement of his dormitory, and impressing buddies as the social director for his fraternity, he was summoned by the dean and told he needed a break, to refocus. "I got thrown out" is how he characterized it.

Without telling his parents he had been suspended, Jeff took a step few saw coming: in the summer of 1965, he joined the navy, and was stationed in San Diego for his two years of service. By the time he returned east, he held a different, wiser view toward his college opportunity. He met Alison Remy just as he was getting ready to resume life as an undergrad, this time at NYU.

That first date was a smashing success. Alison returned home that night, found her father still up working in his office, and declared: "Dad, I think I've met the man I want to marry."

Her father was considerably less moved. "Don't be silly" was his reply.

A few miles north, Jeff told his mother the very same thing that night.

Alison had an intuition, a burgeoning feeling, about the night, about all connected to it—the man she'd met, the feelings he sparked, the summer fading and the autumn approaching. Even about the date itself.

"I will never forget thinking," she recalled more than four decades later, "this day, it's going to have a special meaning for us. I had a powerful sense about it, not only that we just met on this date, but there was something else that was going to make this an important day for our family . . ." Her voice trailed off.

The year was 1968.

The date was September 11.

She graduated in 1970 with a degree in biology and landed a job in medical research at one of the most prestigious addresses for research in the country, Rockefeller University. Alison was going back to New York.

At Rockefeller, she was assigned to help with lab work on a project led by Dr. Vincent Dole and his wife, Dr. Marie Nyswander, who were pioneering the use of a new treatment for heroin addiction. The couple had developed a synthetic medication, methadone, to reduce the intensely painful symptoms of withdrawal that so many addicts experienced in trying to get clean. At the time, addiction was widely seen as something other than a medical problem, viewed through a moral lens, as a defect of character. The doctors rejected that notion and pioneered the use of methadone to help addicts wean themselves from heroin. For his work, Dole would receive the Lasker Award, one of the greatest honors in American medicine.

Alison was working on lab experiments with mice and rats,

injecting the rodents with radioactive methadone to track the effects over a span of months. She was also dating. And on a ferry ride to Martha's Vineyard in the fall of 1970, Jeff proposed. The wedding was the first day of May 1971.

They moved to an apartment in Hastings-on-Hudson, a quaint village in Westchester, and began a life together, Jeff as a banker and Alison continuing as a research assistant. They wanted to start a family, but it took awhile to happen. Alison stopped working at Rockefeller in 1976, to avoid any further exposure to the radioactivity in her lab. Later that year, she and Jeff told the family the news. Alison was expecting.

The slide show still plays in the father's head, a perpetual reel. No conscious decision clicks its carousel to life or chooses the sequence; there's no beam to ignite the dust floating between lens and screen. There is no screen at all, no place outside his head to play the slides. The pictures explode across the sides of his mind, sometimes with enough force to tighten his chest and steal his breath.

Every frame contains his son. A boy blossoming, awkward and beautiful, unfolding into his own life. Rarely are the portraits from milestones, from the passages through the razor wire of adolescence, the first Communions and junior proms, the formal poses and family events, the birthday parties and holiday dinners. Those have moved to the background somehow.

The father can't stop the show, even if he wants to. He knows he won't ever keep them away. The visions come, uninvited and beyond any governing, a tax on his sorrow. The pictures thrill and sear him, comfort and afflict him.

The picture just now is the first frame in a short movie. The son is just *a toddler, not even three years old. He is down on the floor in the living room, playing with the family dog. The two wrestle over a toy, which is the dog's property, the dog biting and the boy pulling, each holding on with all his might. The dog is bigger, stronger. From room to room, the father watches as the dog drags his son around, both wild with delight, neither willing to let go. They play until each is exhausted.*

At times when the boy's grip weakens, his balance falters, and he slides into furniture and crashes into walls. But in the picture in the father's head, the boy won't stop, or cry, or look for help. In his tiny movie, flashing frame by frame, his son goes right back at the dog, until the dog is too tired to keep fighting. The game always ends the same way, with the toy in the boy's hands.

He knew what he wanted to do, and to be.

From the time Welles was in preschool, when he was asked about his future, he had an immediate and confident answer: he would be a fireman. Not like the ones in children's books, but like the people who shared his name and his house. From the time he was a tyke, both his grandfathers would take him to the firehouses in their respective cities—Alison's father, Frank, to the red-tiled, brick-faced, double-doored Fire Station No. 2 in Hartsdale; Jeff's father, Bosley (whom the grandchildren called "Geeps"), to the firehouse in White Plains, just a few blocks from his house. They made the visits not because they were volunteers themselves; they saw the shine in their grandson's eyes, and fed his wonder.

Welles also liked to spend time with Geeps in his home office, "playing business," as the boy called it, hiking himself up behind his grandfather's enormous desk in the sunroom, where Bosley would spend time writing. The interest in business would also last through most of his life. But it was an interest. Something to do. Not something to *be*. It wasn't firefighting.

The fireman's ideal was a magnet for Welles, as it is for so many boys of a certain age. The jubilant blast of the siren, the unpredictable call in the night, the monstrous gleam of the ladder truck, the fearsome power of the hose guns, the boots and turnouts and helmets, and the real and irresistible pull of fire—its brilliance and drama and danger. A living thing, a real and attacking beast. The appeal lay in all of it, and something more, the chance to live out and execute an edict every child is taught but most forget fast: to help.

Christmas 1981, when Welles was four, his grandparents had a special gift for him, a blazing red ride-on fire truck. Upon first seeing it, Welles, who was formally dressed for the holiday in his little Eton suit, stood back for a few moments, as if uncertain how to proceed.

"He was afraid to go near it," Alison said, picturing the scene. "He couldn't believe it was real. He was just so in awe of his fire truck. Maybe he was trying to figure out how they shrunk the truck down." So Welles simply stared at the small metal engine, with its black wheels and bright chrome and beckoning seat behind the steering wheel. How did Santa get it down the chimney? Eventually, he walked toward it, sat down in it, and attempted to maneuver it around the room.

"He climbed in and tried to pedal it," Alison said. "It was not easy to pedal."

The pedals were indeed difficult to crank, and soon the gleaming red sides wore a coat of dust. Even though Welles would ride it at times down the sloped driveway, screaming with joy, wild to the world, he outgrew its small frame soon enough, and the toy

went downstairs in a corner of the house somewhere, ignored and unused.

But the memory of the day, of the gift beside the tree and Welles under its spell, remains.

Welles came by his passion honestly. After all, it was an inheritance.

As it was for his father, one he came into as a teenager during a New England summer. Jeff was out for a drive on Martha's Vineyard, where his family spent a long stretch each summer. While cruising through the Vineyard town of Chilmark, daydreaming, enjoying the freedom that came with his new driver's license, he was snapped out of his reverie by the bark of an order. It was Ozzie Fischer, island tribal elder, waving for him to pull over. Ozzie was a Vineyard treasure to most who knew him. Born in 1914, he'd spent his entire life on the island, a farmer, a town selectman, a local sage. He was also the fire chief in Chilmark.

"Boy," he said, standing next to the driver's door. "Do you have a license? Are you sixteen?"

"Yes."

"Okay," Fischer said. "On Saturday, I will see you down at the firehouse. We need more volunteers. So you are going to volunteer."

Jeff wasn't sure an answer was required, but said yes anyway.

The order was not a surprise. Jeff's two older brothers had already volunteered for the department in summers past; it was the younger one's turn. He would spend the next two years serving. "We didn't get much training" was how he remembered the preparation.

The work was more grimy than dramatic, and Jeff loved it. The most common calls on the island were for dump fires or, indoors, for chimney fires caused by tourists. Visitors could prove overly eager for the romance of a fire on a damp and cool day, without bothering to check whether the flue was open or the chimney actually worked. There were a few of those each summer, smoky affairs that rarely threatened any real damage to the summer cottages. He didn't face a house fire during his time, but the excitement of getting the calls, putting on the gear, rushing to the scenes—that he could remember; and the rush of what might happen and the difference he could make—that stuck inside him. For years, working at his banking career, he lived in towns where there were paid firefighters, and the opportunity to volunteer wasn't there.

A few decades later, in 1985, the chance finally came. The family had been living in Upper Nyack, New York, for a few years by then. Day after day, Jeff passed the perfect little firehouse on

North Broadway. He loved the place—its corner bell tower, its single engine door, its ancient red brick. The building loomed there, a marker from another time, resolute and ready. How many times did he consider stopping in? He always had the next commute to make, or an errand to run. It was around the corner, but he'd never visited.

In September of that year, on a Sunday morning after services, Jeff was in the back hall of the church having coffee when he saw Homer Wanamaker, the chief of police for Orangetown, near the village of Upper Nyack. The two were neighbors. Jeff asked what he knew about the firehouse around the corner. Homer knew plenty.

"I'm president," he said.

Jeff explained his experience out on the Vineyard years ago, and his interest in volunteering.

"Stop off at my house," Homer said. "I'll give you an application."

By November he was voted in. By December, he was cooking a meal for the entire active company, more than two dozen firefighters. Such duty was required of its newest member. He now belonged to Empire Hook and Ladder Company No. 1 of Upper Nyack.

Nyack, New York, is actually composed of five villages and hamlets: Nyack itself and Central, South, West, and Upper Nyack. It was named for the Native Americans who settled the land before the Europeans arrived; the Nyacks migrated north from Coney Island (the word *nyack* in the Algonquin language means "land at the point," and Coney Island does resemble a peninsula at low tide) and moved some thirty miles, to the hillsides that form the riverside terrain of the villages. Situated along the west bank of the Hudson, with a shoreline that looks east, through the erector set of the Tappan Zee Bridge, across to Tarrytown and Westchester County, Nyack's town center grew in step with New York City's residential and industrial sprawl northward.

As jobs and population grew, so did the demands for local government. In 1872, Upper Nyack broke off to form its own incorporated village.

By the count of the 2010 U.S. census, a little more than two thousand people called the village home. Many who live there would say they hail from Nyack, period—the division between Upper and the rest of the Nyacks is important to some, but rarely comes up outside the area's own parochial conversations, and any deeper divisions have largely faded over time.

There are still handsome stone mansions along the river's edge of North Broadway in Upper Nyack, and more modest homes drifting up the hills to the west, looking down on exactly one grocery store, one bar, two synagogues, and one former Christian house of worship, the Old Stone Church, which is owned by the village itself. The First Methodist Episcopal Church of Nyack, the structure's more decorous name, was built over a couple of years from the native stones and timbers of the region and finished in 1813. It's the oldest church building in Rockland County, New York, and is listed on the National Register of Historic Places.

There is a second building on that register: that firehouse at 330 North Broadway. It is a two-story brick structure in the Queen Anne style, finished in the summer of 1887, with a white steeple above its corner bell tower and a gabled façade over its wide door. It has been home to hundreds of village men who have spent

thousands of hours there, arguing and laughing, cooking and eating, remembering and dreaming, and waiting for the bell to ring.

And when it did, the Upper Nyack Firehouse convulsed with
movement. And the volunteers of Empire Hook and Ladder Company No. 1 acted with the resolute urgency of those driven to
reach one destination: wherever the fire was.

The Upper Nyack fire company was formed in 1863, nine years
before the village itself was incorporated. Which is some-
what odd. The village of Nyack already existed, had its own fire
department, and there was no evidence of that department's in-
eptitude. By the standards of the time, Nyack's firemen covered
the region competently. But the men who lived along North
Broadway in what would become Upper Nyack wanted to have the
first and closest chance to save their own families, and their own
homes, in their own way. They wanted the responsibility, and the
honor, of keeping those around them safe. The job was theirs to
do, not someone else's. This mission was the very foundation of
Empire from its charter, its call to existence, instilled in every
firefighter who would ever wear its turnouts.

An insurance claim that reached the New York State Supreme
Court in 1887 suggested, however, that for all its brio, Empire
Hook and Ladder was not infallible. The claim was for fire dam-
age, of all things, to the building occupied by Empire Company
No. 1 itself. The department's own fire station had burned to the
ground, along with its truck.

But by the time the insurance claim was paid in 1888, the new
firehouse for Empire Hook and Ladder was already finished. A
resident of the village who made his fortune out west by selling

supplies to prospectors in the California gold rush was the primary benefactor in funding the new firehouse, with help from other village families. The building took two years to complete.

This time, all parties involved made a simple decision when it came to the new firehouse. The design could be subject to debate, but not the material. There, the choice was clear.

Brick.

B efore they moved to Upper Nyack, the Crowthers lived just to the north, in Pomona, New York. Their house on Ormian Drive had four bedrooms and a flat backyard of maybe half an acre backing up to a patch of woods. They would soon be five: Mom, Dad, Welles, his younger sister, five-year-old Honor, and the baby girl to be, Paige. It was a family's starting point, a two-story base camp from which to strive and grow.

In time, Alison and Jeff Crowther would move the thirteen miles south to Upper Nyack, closer to the city, for various reasons, including proximity to the church where they worshipped. But they were still in Pomona in the winter of 1984, on a cold Sunday morning as they were getting dressed for church, when a father and his seven-year-old son had a conversation about the difference between fashion and function.

Faith was meaningful in the Crowther family. It was not an ornament to display, or a verse to memorize. It was important, if not eclipsing, central but not total. The standards of a Christian upbringing provided a path to living and, if followed, a glorious destination in the end, but there was a lot to do in between, and not all of it among the pews, or on one's knees.

Still, Sunday morning was a clear and holy time in the house;

the first half of the day was devoted to church: dressing for it, getting to it, and attending it.

Welles's wardrobe was the subject between father and son on that winter morning in 1984. As with any question of what it meant to be a man, Welles looked unblinkingly to the same source seeking the same voice: his father.

With time dwindling and the church hour approaching, Welles called for his father's help. He was wearing a new suit, the first Alison had ever bought him, a boy's gray flannel, warm and formal, Sunday best. Welles wanted to complete the ensemble by wearing a tie. But there was a wide gap between desire and ability. After a number of tries, he did what any reasonable boy might do. He shouted down the hall.

"Dad!"

Jeff came, took a knee, flipped up his son's collar, and went to work. As he did, Welles looked down at his father, already dressed and set, and noticed a part of his wardrobe for the first time. Sticking up in a few sharp points in perfect white spikes, he saw the perfection of his father's pocket square.

"What's that, Dad?" he asked. "Can I have one of those?"

"This?" Jeff answered, looking down at his jacket pocket. "Sure."

After cinching the knot up toward the top button of Welles's shirt, Jeff stood up and went back to his bedroom, looking for another white handkerchief. He kept a stash in his top drawer. He reached for one, and at the last second, anticipating where that clean white handkerchief might end up, he grabbed another from his drawer before heading back down the hall to Welles.

When he returned, he bent down again, and showed his son two handkerchiefs in his hands, one white, one red.

He took the white handkerchief and folded it into the same pattern as his own, with the small points projecting upward, neat and sharp. Instantly, it took shape, like a pressed piece of origami. He tucked it into the small breast pocket of Welles's suit coat, and made sure the presentation matched his.

"Well," Jeff said, "that's for show." Welles smiled.

Then he pulled out the other handkerchief he'd carried into the room.

He looked at Welles and smiled, holding out a red bandanna.

"This," said Jeff, "is for blow." He made a gesture, holding it up toward his face. "To blow your nose."

He made sure Welles understood the difference, and then folded the red handkerchief neatly and placed it in the back right pocket of his son's pants.

"You can always keep this back there," Jeff told him. "You'll always have it if you need it."

"Thank you, Daddy," Welles said, beaming. "That's great." In the simple course of getting dressed, the boy had received this unexpected gift.

During the services at Grace Episcopal, Welles stood straight, looked handsome, and felt proud. He was a portrait in his new suit. But it was the bandanna in his pocket, tucked inside with just the top edge peeking out, that gave his wardrobe that extra bit of flash, to carry and keep.

The red bandanna would have other uses in time. To wipe away sweat and dirt, or clean up a mess, or keep the hair out of his eyes. Or to polish up a bumper or a gleaming silver bell. The handkerchief was a welcome sight, especially during the endless cleaning and polishing that went into the firehouse day. Or when a parade loomed on the calendar, and many would after Jeff joined Empire. For every firehouse in Nyack, the town parade meant two things: an all-out war of pride in having the cleanest rig, and the tedious process of making it that way.

Empire Hook and Ladder's volunteers wanted every piece of chrome blinding, every rim shining, every inch gleaming. The challenge for every ladder truck was the same: a lot of inches to cover, and a lot of them in places never meant to shine, or even to reach.

For this inglorious labor, the company had a special worker who was adored for his ethic.

"Hey, Welles, do you want to come with me to the firehouse?"

At eight years old, the answer was automatic.

"Yes, Daddy."

He was put to work immediately. Welles already knew many of the men as his father's friends, seeing them at church or around town, but in this setting they possessed a different air. Larger, warmer, brighter in their blue T-shirts, they traded inside jokes punctuated by booms of laughter. They were a team. And they had no one to play the position of crawler.

The men had started to remove the ladders from the bed atop the truck, and the space underneath was thick with leaves and sticks and congealed muck and grime.

Who exactly was going to crawl in there?

"Welles, you want to?"

The boy jumped right up to the top of the truck and crawled forward, his feet disappearing from view before being replaced by a set of hands sticking out from the top of the bed, waiting for the tools he'd need. He was handed a vacuum hose and began sucking out the detritus that the other cleanings and washings and waxings missed. He was eager and happy. The men listened to the vacuum slurp and watched the hose stretch, and shared a hearty laugh. The kid was good. He was useful.

He was one of them.

I n a way, the firehouse was Welles's first team. There would be many others, with different uniforms on different fields. He poured himself into all of them, hearing the same mantras whatever the season.

Effort counts. Attitude matters. Hard work wins.

Welles took them all in—the nostrums and platitudes rarely given to the naturally talented, who don't need to hear them, at least not yet. The encouragements and clichés were delivered to him from the start, and accepted as gospel. Of course the world yielded to effort. The victory always belonged to the most determined. How could a result be shaped any differently?

From the time he began to play sports, Welles epitomized the try-hard guy, the striver, the kid wringing out whatever ability he has through practice and will. A streak of fearlessness was useful too, as an available substitute for physical genius.

He taught himself to skateboard when he was nine years old, dangerous enough for a boy whose house sat near the bottom of a large hill in town. The house was also a venue for the monotonous thud of plastic hockey pucks on summer mornings, blasted into the net and the walls beyond. Neighborhood kids heard the sound for hours on end.

As he first entered the civilization of youth sports, he found that he simply loved being on a team in all the sports he played—football, baseball, hockey, lacrosse. So often, *team* is the refuge of the effort and glue guys, the ones whose instincts for the game outpace any selfish flair, players who work for the good of the whole because they understand what the more brilliant player may never grasp: a good whole allows everyone, the good and the not as good, to get better.

Before concentrating on hockey and then lacrosse exclusively, Welles played on Pop Warner football teams for several seasons, moving up each year by grade and weight. His lack of size became more conspicuous as the weight divisions grew wider, with a greater range of players competing against one another.

As one of the smaller ten- or eleven-year-olds in his grade, Welles played defensive back for the Valley Cottage Indians. In Oklahoma drills, where two players went head to head with each other in close quarters, a contact drill where each is trying to knock the other down, Welles was a tough out. Matt Drowne, a bigger teammate, remembered the drills vividly. "He was a genuinely tough kid," Drowne said. "I think of him knocking the s— out of me."

He became part of a group called "the mosquito defense." The name fit—a bunch of light, quick players who took pride in being pests. Persistent, annoying, buzzing around the ball. In their Pop Warner league that year, the team went undefeated—and, to the great joy of the mosquitoes, unscored upon—to win their league title.

He wanted a sleepover at the house to celebrate his eleventh birthday. About ten boys on a Friday night, eating pizza and watching movies, talking about sports and laughing at one another's fart jokes. What could go wrong?

Jeff smiled seeing Welles's collection of buddies coming through the door, from a few down the street who were a couple of years older to the brothers Dickie and Alexander Perry to longtime pals like Jon Hess. The smartest boy in the class, Jonathan Sperman, made the gang for the night as well.

Alison was away on a business trip, leaving Jeff in charge. No heavy lifting. Have some pizza delivered, set out the snacks and soda, get a stack of VHS titles, and herd the boys downstairs into the finished basement—plenty of floor space to spread out the sleeping bags and blankets for the night. *Dragnet,* the 1987 movie with Tom Hanks and Dan Aykroyd, was selected as the marquee feature.

Jeff was smart enough to set himself upstairs, alert for any disturbing sounds, reading the paper on the couch. He made his last check on the boys shortly after ten P.M., when the movie was just getting started. All settled in for the night, including Dad.

Jeff slept soundly on the couch, the paper folded by his side, until snapping awake at nearly two A.M. He swung his feet down to the floor and headed toward the basement to check on the sleeping boys.

The lights were all on; that was odd. He walked down the stairs. There was not a towheaded middle schooler to be found. The sleeping bags and blankets were as empty as the room. No one was there.

Jeff ran back up the stairs. He began flying around the house, not calling out—he didn't want to wake the girls, who were asleep in their rooms (thanks be to God). He started opening closet doors, looking in the shower tub, even peering into the larger kitchen cabinets. No trace. No boys.

Just then, he saw a prick of light out the windows looking over the deep backyard. Then another, and another. Small, weak beams were sweeping across the grass and into the trees, pointing in opposite directions. He rushed outside and heard the voices. The boys.

"Welles Crowther!" First and last name. Never good. "Get here NOW!"

Welles came across the yard to the back of house. His father tried very hard to hide the swell of relief and maintain a proper degree of outrage.

"Dad, we were playing flashlight tag and . . ."

"Do you know what time it is?!"

Welles admitted he knew only that it was late.

"All you boys! In the house right away. Get inside and get downstairs . . ."

The boys came quickly, sweaty and flushed.

"Now," Jeff said, "keep quiet and get downstairs. Get in those sleeping bags. Lights out immediately."

They bounded through the house and down to the basement, Jeff behind them. Each went straight to his part of the floor, and once they were in their sleeping bags or under their blankets, Jeff gave a last stern look, walked up the stairs, and turned off the light.

Flashlight tag? At two in the morning? He swallowed a smile as he made his way to bed.

Morning came, the boys left, the episode went unmentioned. Until a few days later, when Welles came to his father, a pained look on his face. He wanted to talk.

"Dad," he began, "the other night during the sleepover, when you came out to the backyard . . . we didn't just play flashlight tag."

Jeff hadn't forgotten, but the panic had long receded.

Welles explained. When Jeff came out to the backyard, the boys were actually returning from a bigger adventure. After the movie finished, they were not ready for sleep. Someone suggested heading over to their old elementary school, where several temporary classrooms had been erected. The buildings were close to the boys' real destination, the roof over the school's large all-purpose room, used as a gymnasium, auditorium, and lunchroom. Vast and flat, the roof held a schoolboy's treasure: all the lost tennis balls, baseballs, rubber balls, and footballs thrown errantly across its space, collecting up there over a few months' time, never to be returned to sender.

The roof was flat but more than two stories high, reaching twenty-five feet. It was used by the volunteers at Empire for ladder training. A fall back onto the schoolyard would mean a trip to a hospital, at the least. The boys found a route up to the gym rooftop using a walkway attached to the modular classrooms. One by one the boys made their way up, Welles near the back of the line, hesitant. Sperman, the class brain, was last and refused to go, noting the danger and urging Welles to stay with him. Welles knew his friend was right, that it was foolish to go up, but all the other boys were already up, running around, scavenging for balls. Welles gave in and made the climb, leaving Sperman behind.

With their collection secure, they made their way down, across the schoolyard and through the darkened streets, into the Crowthers' backyard. That's when the game of flashlight tag commenced.

After explaining what happened, Welles looked at his father, understanding that this was his first experience with peer pressure and its powers, and ashamed for having caved in to it. He didn't need the balls. He wasn't searching for the thrill. The need for approval put him on the roof.

He wasn't relieved after telling the truth. He was waiting for Dad's shoe to drop.

"What kind of punishment do you think you should get?" Jeff asked.

Welles didn't hesitate. "No TV for two months," he said.

Jeff dismissed it out of hand. Too severe.

"How about two *weeks* instead?"

The defendant accepted. Happily.

E*leven.* Where does that age fall? Both feet still planted firmly in the grass of boyhood, but starting to peer over the fence, to pull gently away from the absolute rule of home, to examine its laws—deciding when to apply and what to obey, and which to amend or ignore.

For Welles, it was also a time to have a taste of bullying, that phenomenon as old as schooling itself. Boys, like little nation-states in blue jeans and striped shirts, tested one another. Some were neutral, some targets, others aggressors.

Bullying wasn't the catchall term yet, however. *Picked on* was the phrase most often used to speak to what happened. More simply put, it was cruelty. Petty, timeless, endemic to childhood, and rarely acknowledged or stopped. So it was for Welles.

In time he would grow into his body, not only fast but strong, rounding out as an athlete, but that time was still a ways off. He would never grow to be imposing in a purely physical way, but his frame would broaden, adding bulk and sinew. Welles wasn't the biggest in anything, really—not in his classes, among his friends, or on his teams. For a while growing up he'd be the opposite—smaller and shorter than teammates, undersized compared with friends and peers.

His sister Honor, younger by two years, remembered an excruciating period when they were both in middle school and, for just a few months, she was a bit taller. He hated being the shorter brother. And every chance he got to deliver kid punches to her arms, he brought the sting. She remembers the small bruises and Welles's smiles afterward. The lack of size invited a range of reactions and responses. He handled the ribbing as best he could, up to a point. Like most kids who endure their moments of being teased, he kept his feelings inside. It was a rare wall erected between him and his parents. His mom and dad didn't know how much the pestering bothered him.

As he entered middle school, many of the boys in his grade were head and shoulders taller than Welles. He wasn't yet five feet tall. One bigger boy in particular used the bus rides with Welles to and from school to badger him. They'd board the bus near the bottom of Birchwood Avenue and N. Midland in the village. A crossing guard stood sentry at the intersection, protecting the students in their comings and goings, but also serving as witness to their alliances and disputes.

It wasn't the crossing guard who called. It was the president of the PTA, a friend named Rikke Stone. Working at the time as a saleswoman for an upscale women's clothing line, Alison was out of the house, covering part of her territory in Long Island, when she answered the call.

Apparently, Stone was driving up Birchwood, past the Crowthers' house, and saw two boys fighting on the front lawn. Well, it wasn't a fight, really. More like a pummeling, at least as Stone reported it. Welles was the boy throwing the blows.

"Pounding on him," Alison heard from Stone. And then heard it again. "Pound, pound, pound."

Alison was baffled. The only details she got were the plainest: Welles was on the front lawn of the family house on top of another boy and hitting him repeatedly. She knew she needed to get home and talk to her son.

After getting back to Upper Nyack, she saw that Welles was unhurt, and in fact unmarked. He was calm.

"Welles," she asked, "what on earth happened? Who is this kid?"

"He swung at me with his lunch box," Welles said. "He was swinging at my head. So that's when I just took him down."

The crossing guard at the intersection would corroborate Welles's story. She had watched the tension building between the boys, and described it to the school administrators. She sensed the fuse.

"Mrs. Crowther," she said, "that boy picked on Welles every single day. Picked on him, tormented him."

Welles never spoke about any type of bullying with his mother at all, never betrayed that he was being picked on or harassed by another student. She knew her son well, and she knew his friends. But when asked, Welles told her plainly. The crossing guard's account was spot on. He beat the snot out of the other boy.

If there was any glint of pride in her, she hid it. But Alison understood, and inside she approved. She knew that Welles was doing what his father had told him to do. "Don't ever start a fight," Jeff had told his son years before. "But if one starts, be sure you finish it."

After finding out what happened, Alison paid a visit to the boy's mother.

"You've got to get your son to stop this," she said. "He's got to stop picking on my son."

It was maternal instinct guiding her, but unnecessary. Welles had delivered the message on the front lawn with his fists, settling the matter. He would have moments when he would be picked on as he continued through school, but not the same way, and never by the boy he felled on the front lawn.

I t was the sound—the worst the boys had ever heard.

Jon Hess and Keith O'Brien were friends and neighbors to Welles, frequent visitors to the Crowthers' house on Birchwood after school, always ready to play the game of the day. They were competitive with one another, as most young athletes are. The pecking order eventually grew clear. Hess would become the best athlete among them, and among most of the boys his age in Nyack. Strong, fast, and instinctive, he was fluid on a field, a natural performer and leader in multiple sports in town, but lacrosse would become his focus. Later, at Princeton, he would have one of the greatest collegiate careers in the history of the sport, winning three national championships and being named the NCAA tournament's most outstanding player as a junior in 1997. He would go on to play professionally, in the National Lacrosse League and Major League Lacrosse. Welles admired Hess deeply, to the point of idolizing him.

O'Brien, like Hess, was a year older than Welles and a grade ahead of him in school. The two older boys would be his teammates in high school in Nyack, as well as friends after they'd all graduated.

One spring day in 1989 when O'Brien and Hess were thirteen years old and Welles was twelve, they were playing at the back of the Crowthers' driveway when they made the discovery.

The Crowthers had a passion for prize boxers. They entered them in shows and competitions, and doted on them accordingly, as most owners of purebreds do. The dogs were four-legged siblings for the kids. At any given time, there were several purebreds in the house or in the wire-fenced dog run they'd built for the dogs in the yard.

Blazer, the male, was older now and no longer ready for show, but the family kept him at Welles's urging. He was Welles's dog more than the others. There were two female boxers in the brood as well, Molly and Socks. They were all outside in the dog run that day as the boys played.

Over their own shouts from the driveway, none of the boys heard or saw exactly what happened. But at some point, one of them noticed the evidence. Apparently, a groundhog had lost its balance on the retaining wall above the dog run and fallen into the pen. On instinct, the dogs attacked, mauling the animal. The boys found one of its detached limbs, a leg, lying just beyond the fence.

The groundhog was barely able to escape, wedging itself between a gutter pipe and a retaining wall where the dogs could no longer reach it. Bleeding heavily from the stump where its leg had been ripped away, the animal breathed wildly, unable to move.

The boys were stricken by the sight. They tried not to hear the yelps, or look at the fresh wound. They turned to one another. *What do we do?*

Welles went inside the house and called his father.

"Dad," he said, "there's a groundhog that got into the dog run, and the dogs went after it and chewed on it."

"How bad is it?" Jeff asked.

"Bad."

"Well, then," Jeff said, "you've got to put it out of its misery."

Welles didn't understand.

"You have that aluminum bat, the one you used to play Little League?"

"Yes," Welles said.

"Take the dogs out of the run, put them in the house, and then use the bat. Hit the animal on the head."

Welles now understood what his father meant. He hung up the phone, found the bat, and came back outside, where Hess and O'Brien were waiting. He told his friends his father's instruction. He didn't offer the bat to either of them, nor did they ask for it. They could still hear the animal's moans and, when they forced themselves to look, still see the blood.

Welles began to cry as he walked to the spot where the groundhog lay, wounded and trapped. He raised the bat, brought it down on the animal's head with a sickening crunch, the noise of bone shattering, and then did it again. Blood smeared the barrel of the bat and splattered, spraying upward toward Welles's face. He struck down on the animal's skull half a dozen times or more.

"Keith and I were cowering in the corner, not even looking," Hess said, remembering the scene outside the house. "One swing of the bat, and we covered our eyes and didn't want to see anything anymore. . . . The sound was, it was breaking bones, there was blood. Welles was standing now, in full tears, swinging the bat. It was very difficult for him to do that."

O'Brien remembered it clearly as well. "It was traumatic for me," he said. "You're a kid. It's not something you see, that kind of brutality. . . . It was something that had to be done, and he was the only one man enough to step up and do it."

After the final blows, Welles paused for a moment, and then went back inside the house to call his father.

"I did it," Welles said, in tears. Jeff could hear his son breathing hard through the line.

"You did the right thing," his father told him. A short time later, Jeff left the office and made his way home. When he got there, he found the groundhog's shattered body, picked it up with a shovel, and carried it to the far edge of the backyard. He dug a small hole and buried it there. Welles didn't watch his father, and didn't ask what he'd done with the remains.

Beyond the last phone call, neither mentioned it again.

Small, at five feet two inches and just over a hundred pounds, Welles still entered high school with a certain self-assurance—he was a good athlete, getting better, and a strong student on an honors track. Still, there were those who mocked him, sometimes good-naturedly and to his face, other times harshly and behind his back. He was different in ways easily spotted, even if he spent less time dwelling on the differences than others did. He was no rebel, nor was he caught up in anyone else's desire to conform.

One of the easiest targets was his wardrobe. In the early nineties, as the grunge scene took over suburban America, Nyack was no different. Ripped jeans and heavy flannels were the uniform of the day. Not for Welles.

Michael Barch, a classmate and buddy, remembered the style years later. "He was the opposite," Barch said. "L.L. Bean, Vineyard Vines. Nyack was old, grungy, plaid. Welles was wearing Polo shirts."

Keith O'Brien, who played hockey with Welles, remembered a time earlier when he got a new bag to carry all his gear—the skates, sticks, and pads that came along with the sport. The bags were massive, with handles large enough to slip over a player's shoulder, perfect as a prop to use in a prank where Welles was the target.

"We used to always make fun of Welles because he was so small," said O'Brien. "We bet Welles, 'I bet you can't fit in the bag.' So of course we got Welles to go into the hockey bag. Well, once you put him in the bag and zipped him up, what's the next thing you do?"

They looked to test the limits of the bag and its human cargo.

"We lifted the bag and threw him down my stairs," O'Brien said. "I remember that he fit into the hockey bag, and once we got him in there we said, okay, he is going down." Welles emerged unhurt and, according to O'Brien, wasn't a crybaby, in this case, or any other he could remember.

In every high school, one can make a list of the names of students no one would test or mock. Welles never made any such list. Even his car was a target. It was a decidedly uncool van/box truck contraption, teenage self-consciousness on four wheels if ever there was such a vehicle. The truck had its bumper torn off and a screeching backup safety beeper that emitted sound levels somehow higher and more shrill than a car alarm. Jody Steinglass, a classmate, remembered the echo, and the mockery it inspired. "It beeped when you put it in reverse," he said. "When he pulled away from a party, it was BEEP-BEEP-BEEP. . . . I would've died if I had that car."

The vehicle was an endless source of derision, which Welles accepted and laughed at for its obvious truth.

I n the landscape of youth sports, there will always be a special place for the hockey family. While other games require only an open field or a dirt diamond or a hoop on a pole, hockey needs more—a lot more, starting with ice. Sure, there are frozen ponds aplenty in Canada and Scandinavia, and more than a few in New England and Minnesota, and even some in Rockland County. But by and large around New York City's suburbs, the game is played indoors, in half-freezing warehouses on oval-shaped rinks.

There is no sunny side of the stands for spectators or shady dugouts to fill, no spring breezes to enjoy, only the stale cold air and the empty hum of the overhead fluorescents. You don't play hockey, or drive through the dark freeze of winter mornings to watch it, because it's easy. For the vast majority of Americans, it will never be the game of choice. You don't play it by default. Skating is not just running. It's running across sheets of hoarfrost. The first fundamental is balance, and only after that's mastered does a player receive a stick, and then a puck on its end. The ice is a cold floor to receive your fall, and young players fall often and land hard.

Welles also played the easier games, but hockey held a special place for him. He was still undersized, but his coordination and effort lent him a quickness, a burst that served him and at times separated him. The game was physical and often reckless, with players crashing into the boards and one another, and the collisions gave the atmosphere a dash of chaos. From his first few games and practices, he was an elusive skater, able to navigate his way around traffic and avoid the big hits.

By his freshman year at Nyack High School, he was playing varsity, spending his time with the bigger boys, ready to compete in games. He played right wing—a glamour position, where a player earns looks at the net and chances to score if he flashes into the spaces where the puck is *going* to be.

Welles played smart and hard, his skill and speed developing. By the start of his junior year, he saw himself as a leader, but when coach Dave Moreno named the team's captains before the season, Welles wasn't chosen. Two other teammates, Matt Dickey and Chris Varmon, were selected. The same day, Welles sought out Moreno.

"Coach," he said, "can we talk about something?"

"Sure."

"I'm curious. I want to know what I'm doing wrong."

Moreno understood immediately Welles was talking about the captaincy.

"What do I have to do?"

There were many ways for Moreno to answer. Clearly, his player was disappointed, hurt, even. But Welles came to him directly, without sulking or taking an attitude, or becoming a divisive presence in the locker room. He wanted to know. The coach's answer was clear.

"It's not what you're doing wrong," Moreno said. "It's just . . . there's *more*. You're a leader by example. But you can do *much more*."

"Okay," Welles said, turned around, and left.

His response came on the ice, in how he talked to other players, and in how he challenged other teammates in the locker room, to care about each shift with the same intensity and effort, and to hold one another accountable when their effort flagged. The team's ultimate goal wasn't only to win but to move up the rungs of the league, to face greater competition.

The coach watched to see how Welles would react to the snub. He listened as the voice grew louder and the demands sharper. He was impressed. Two weeks later, Moreno called Welles in to see him. The meeting was short.

He placed a large C on Welles's Nyack Indians jersey, naming him the team's third captain.

That year the team had 10 wins and 2 losses in league play, Welles turning a sharp wrist shot from the circle into a key weapon. He also used the shot as a ploy in developing a role he'd refine late in his tenure on the team. Toward the end of his career, he became known to the younger players as the veteran most willing to help them get their first goals for the Indians. When a player was still searching for the net, he asked Moreno to put him on his line. Off the right wing, Welles would sweep in with a move to shoot, but then flip the puck across him to a teammate he'd set up, having instructed him ahead of time to trail the play down the middle of the ice. When the play worked, the goalie unable to adjust in time and change direction, the teammate would redirect the pass into the net for his first career score. Welles would fly past, retrieve the puck, and bring it to the bench as a keepsake for his teammate.

By his senior year, when the Indians played some of their games against League 1 opponents—the highest level of competition—the team finished with 6 wins, 5 losses, and 2 ties.

With the red bandanna tied around his head, worn beneath his helmet in every game, Welles was one of the section's leading scorers.

Christmas morning, 1993.

Into the holy silence shrouding the house, indifferent to the gifts wrapped beneath the tree and the plans for church and feast and family, the call came, its shrill notes bleating out from Jeff's beeper. The annunciator device he kept in the house spoke in minimalist code.

Signal 10. Working fire—to be worked by father and son, together. It was Welles's first fire call.

Two years earlier, Welles finally asked the question Jeff had long awaited. His son wanted to apply to become a junior firefighter, to start down the path toward joining him at Empire Hook and Ladder as more than a company mascot and ready hand. He wanted to answer the call. Welles was fourteen, still too young in his father's view. Jeff told him he needed to be sixteen before he could apply and begin training. Two years later, shortly after his sixteenth birthday, Welles asked again. Dad agreed.

Welles completed the county's firefighter training program that summer, learning the fundamentals of fire prevention and suppression, and spending time in the county's "smoke house," putting out supervised fires. He was hungry to start. He'd seen his father rush off to fires since he was a boy, and wanted to join him. This Christmas morning was his chance.

Jeff was out of bed, slipping pants on and looking for a shirt. He often slept with his socks on in case an alarm sounded overnight, but apparently the trick wasn't saving enough time. Welles heard the beeper go off from his bedroom below and was dressed instantly, and now he was exhorting his father to step on it.

"Dad," he shouted up the stairs. "Better hurry up!"

Without a second glance they passed the tree and the spread of gifts beneath and pushed out the door. Jeff flipped on the blue flashing lights on the dashboard of his truck and they made the turn to Empire. They were too late; the truck was already gone. The dispatcher sent out the call in more detail, a structure fire in Grand View-on-Hudson. Lights blinking, they raced to the address a little more than three miles south, directly on the river.

They caught sight of Empire's truck before getting there, and followed behind to the scene. The flames were plainly visible through the windows of the house.

Grand View-on-Hudson, a tiny village of less than a quarter of a square mile, was best known for its homes directly on the west bank of the Hudson, giving the hamlet of fewer than three hundred residents its name. The house on fire was more than a picturesque river cottage. It belonged to the most famous person in town, Toni Morrison.

At sixty-two years old, she'd returned from Stockholm two weeks earlier after receiving the Nobel Prize in Literature. A giant of American letters, the author of *Song of Solomon, The Bluest Eye,* and *Jazz,* she'd won the Pulitzer Prize in 1988 for the novel *Beloved.*

Morrison wasn't at home. Since 1989, she spent most of her time an hour and a half south, living and teaching in Princeton as a professor of creative writing. The house in Grand View-on-Hudson was primarily a retreat, and a beautiful one. Now it was ablaze. Morrison's son Slade was alone in the house at the time the fire started, and according to police, he'd tried to react when an ember leaped from the fireplace and landed on a nearby couch, igniting it. He moved to tamp down the sparks, but quickly the flames mounted, growing out of control. He called the fire department, and within minutes, the four-story wooden Colonial was nearly engulfed.

Jeff and Welles pulled up to a home overwhelmed by flames, drawing roughly a hundred firefighters to the scene. The two reported to the captain seeking instruction. Welles was dispatched with a third lieutenant to the side of the house, to assist with ventilation efforts. Jeff watched him walk to the edge of the riverside property and disappear. Whatever worries he had about his son crossing the bridge from training to task were meaningless now. Welles was on the line, in the company, answering the call, a responder. Besides, Jeff had his own assignment to handle in the front of the house as the fight wore on.

Slade escaped unhurt. The house, however, contained precious material. A portion of Toni Morrison's original manuscripts and other writings were inside, invaluable works of art on the most fragile of canvases—paper. The firefighters understood that the priority was to extinguish and contain the flames, but, also urgently, to preserve the works and treasures of an American master.

Ultimately, the effort would last more than five hours before the fire was put down. A few of the firefighters sustained minor injuries. The house was gutted by the fire, but the manuscripts and writings survived intact. It helped that they'd been stored in a special study in the house, with some extra measure of fire protection.

Jeff and Welles crossed paths only once, during a water break, with the fire still alive. By the time it was done, likely they never saw the anxious homeowner at the edge of the property. After her son called her, Morrison rushed north, arriving to see the final stages, and the smoldering shell of her home.

The firefighters received the Signal 14. Return to quarters.

When they got in the truck, Jeff looked over at his son.

"How you doing there?"

"Oh," he said. "I'm great."

The reply was redundant. As the truck pulled away, the smile through the grime was answer enough.

H igh school is closer to the core of the American experience than anything else I can think of," the great American novelist Kurt Vonnegut Jr. once wrote. So many experiences find ready, if unattractive, parallels to what we live through from grades nine to twelve. It's all there: the cliques and stereotypes, the wise and the cruel, the popular and the marginalized, and the first discovery of our pursuits and limits as we take the halting steps into our adult selves. Life is high school without scheduled study hall. Vonnegut's truth was alive and on display in its modern rendering twenty-five years later, in the hallways of Nyack High School.

The old high school, where Welles and his classmates spent some of their middle school years, looked idyllic from the outside. Opened in 1928, the school sat high on a ridge above the Hudson. A two-story Georgian Colonial of red brick and white trim, it easily could've been lifted from the fields of a New England prep school. A clock tower sat at its center, crowned by a cupola. By the time Welles was a freshman, his class was in a new high school, a modern structure of drab brown brick and utilitarian shape. The drop in curb appeal was steep, even though the view from the back athletic fields out to the Hudson could be breathtaking.

But on this particular afternoon in 1995, many students weren't pondering the riverside. They wanted a close-up view of what was about to happen in the hallway. They were watching two students fixing for a fight.

Lee Burns sat directly in front of Welles in Mr. Antonetti's twelfth-grade advanced English class. They were friends and fellow seniors, part of a group who congregated at Karim Raoul's house, a classmate who had his own separate space on his father's property where the boys would gather. It was their spot. Welles was welcomed, but at times failed to blend in entirely.

"We were always at Karim's," Burns said. "People would drink. . . . A lot of us were athletes who maybe had a beer, but we weren't smokers, we weren't into drugs. But there were kids around us who were into those things." It was high school. Kids got drunk and got high, and sometimes got out of control and got themselves into trouble.

The high school had a self-appointed group to limit the damage. VAASA, Varsity Athletes Against Substance Abuse, was a collection of varsity athletes who pledged to be clean and sober. Some of the athletes in the group drank or smoked, and used the extracurricular group to pad their college applications while flouting its mission. To their partying classmates, the group was sometimes viewed as preachy and laughable, the kids who wouldn't be invited to parties anyway but were somehow expected to provide an example to their cool counterparts.

Welles was invited to the parties, at least some of the time, but neither Burns nor others had ever seen him drink. Welles took his role with VAASA seriously, and was the designated driver at every party he attended, according to his friends. Burns never heard him preach to anyone, or sound judgmental, but Welles spoke up when he thought he should. Burns had heard him often, and seen the eye rolls.

The best example he'd seen of Welles's self-imposed sense of duty came whenever there was a fire call.

"The most beautiful girl sitting there," Burns recalled, having seen Welles make his pitch toward a potential date and then hear the fire call. "He's gone. We're having a good time, and that alarm goes off. He went to Superman mode and just went to the call."

This time the bell wasn't sounding any alarm beyond the end of English class. Burns, Welles, and the other students flooded out into the hallways, where Burns spotted his girlfriend, a junior, with another classmate, Wykeme Corker. The scene instantly upset him. Whatever history there was between the two wasn't good, and looking down the hallway, Burns believed Corker was bothering his girlfriend. In his mind, Corker, a sophomore football player, was a serial bully in the school. And now he was acting aggressively toward his girlfriend.

Burns felt a rage building inside him as he saw Corker coming down the hall. He wanted to defend his girlfriend, wanted to confront Corker, and wanted to release the feeling building in his chest. "I just felt something primal inside me," he said.

The floor was filled with students out of class standing at their lockers. Seeing the two approach each other in the hallway, a crowd quickly began to form. They wanted a fight. Burns wasn't going to disappoint them.

"I was prepared to do whatever it took," he said. "In that moment, I was preparing to do something that I would regret the rest of my life." A quarter century later, the tension in his voice was still there.

At what point might a life turn? Can it be in a fight in a high school hallway?

Less than five years after squaring off with Burns in October 1995, Wykeme Corker would get into another confrontation in Nyack, around midnight outside the Signal 13 Bar. He would stab a man in the stomach, slashing the victim's hand, nearly severing his thumb. He was indicted by a Rockland County grand jury and charged with attempted murder and assault. Acquitted of the more serious charge, he was convicted of assault and sentenced in 2000 to twelve and a half years in state prison. He served most of it before being paroled in 2011.

Corker returned to Nyack. Just a few months after his release and a few blocks from the stabbing that sent him to prison, he found trouble again. Outside a social club early on a Saturday morning, he was slashed across the neck with a broken beer bottle. The wounds were fatal. Wykeme Corker died at the age of thirty-three.

There was no way to foretell the darkness ahead for Corker when Burns faced him in the crowded hallway with as many as two hundred students gathering to goad them on. There was also no way for anyone to know what would happen if they charged at each other and tangled. Corker was a football player. Burns was six feet five and well built. Neither was backing up.

Just then, Burns felt a hand on his shoulder and turned, hearing a voice in his ear.

It was Welles.

"Lee," he said. "Think of everything you have to lose. This guy has nothing to lose."

Welles didn't talk to Corker, or even look at him. He spoke only to Burns. He was the only student to approach either one.

"I had this peace come over me," Burns said. "Almost immediately, I could feel my hands releasing, they weren't clenched anymore." Burns turned, found his girlfriend, and without waiting to hear what Corker was saying, he walked away. Welles stayed behind, watching them go.

The crowd, unsatisfied, soon left. In minutes, the hallway was empty.

Years later, when Burns learned of Corker's arrest and then his murder, his mind returned to the hallway and the voice in the din that spoke to him. "It was a crossroad to my life," Burns said. "Truth be told, if he had not said something to me and I would go on to do what I felt I had to do, or what I felt my anger dictated that I should do, I would not be sitting [here] today. I would not be the parent of my daughter. I would not be a lot of things. All because of one young kid . . ."

Burns paused. "I thank him for that."

With Welles's strong grades and high board scores and honor rolls and advanced classes and extracurriculars and varsity letters and captaincy, with his work ethic and firefighting dedication and his family legacy, even with Division I lacrosse talent, it wasn't enough for the Ivy League. Welles wasn't going to Princeton, as his grandfather Bosley did. Where his good friend Jon Hess was a freshman lacrosse player. Where he could pledge a dining club or give Toni Morrison a direct account of how he tried to save her house from burning down.

Instead, he was going to Boston College, a place he'd come to love quickly and play for proudly. The Ivy League would have conferred a prestigious degree, sure. But BC would lead to invaluable connections and memories, and, perhaps, to a hell of a lot more fun.

Before going, Welles left behind that quintessential snapshot of a student's high school experience, the senior yearbook page. His stated ambition? "To make the best of everything, to sail around the world with the woman I love, and to paint my bumper."

H istoric. Idyllic. Gothic.
Private. Sheltered. Favored.

Whatever the archetypal college campus image, Boston College fills out the picture handsomely. The stone towers watching over quadrangles of green, the ivy climbing in witness, the residue of aspiration covering every bench and footpath with dew, it was a place founded through religion and endowed by success. A walk across its campuses reinforces that notion—in the beauty of its buildings, the silence of its libraries, the solemnity of its museums.

Six miles west of downtown, the Chestnut Hill campus covers 175 acres, with more than 120 buildings and halls, draped across a hilltop overlooking its namesake reservoir. Known locally as The Heights, on a fall afternoon or football Saturday its property is as intoxicating and alluring as youth itself, when youth has opportunity to explore, and advantage to exercise.

The class of 1999, more than two thousand strong, arrived on campus in the late summer of 1995 as most freshmen tribes do—high on autonomy, terrified of freedom, and hoping to fit in. There were mixers and orientation, academic registration and class sign-ups. And there were housing assignments, the single largest lottery piece in a student's arrival. A freshman dorm floor is a periodic table, a social experiment governed by forces not yet charted, the interactions impossible to forecast.

Welles was assigned to Duchesne East, not an ideal spot geographically. Duchesne East and West sit among a cluster of dorms on the Newton campus, separated from the heart of the college grounds, and typically requiring a shuttle ride to classes. It was widely seen as the worst of the freshmen spots to draw, and many there put in for housing transfers as quickly as they could, hoping to move to the lower, middle, or upper campus by second semester, to be closer to all things academic and social. Welles wanted to move too, but understood he was stuck for the first semester, at least.

There was an advantage to having a precast identity to rely upon as an incoming freshman. In the first meetings and initial impressions and sizings up that formed the first few weeks of life in college, Welles possessed an answer to the question that came after *Where are you from?* He knew what he was *into,* and at any given moment, he was usually carrying the evidence. Welles came to Boston College to compete in Division I college lacrosse, the sport he loved most and played best. There were other pursuits, of course—earning a degree, finding a girlfriend, building a ramp to a career—but as a freshman those were in the ether, across the other side of four unshaped years. Playing a sport at the highest college level was immediate. Its demands would lend shape to his schedule, purpose to his days, and progress to the calendar. It would also provide a ready-made batch of friends. With sticks.

Johnny Howells, a classmate who would live with Welles in his senior year and become one of his closest friends, remembered the first several times he saw him across campus outside a quadrangle of dorms. Each time, Welles was carrying a lacrosse stick across his shoulder, twirling and spinning it by reflex, its webbing in constant rotation. Howells knew little about the sport, but figured Welles for a good and speedy player, given his lack of size. Welles was still small, five six or five seven and barely 150 pounds.

If not dwarfed by many teammates as an incoming freshman, he was certainly in their shadows.

The Eagles' program wasn't in the same strata as Hess's Princeton, it wasn't a national power, but it was Division I. Despite his size, Welles's tenacity earned him the chance to continue playing.

"Welles got it," said Ed Moy, his lacrosse coach at BC. "He considered it a privilege to play for the Eagles, even though he wasn't on scholarship or on the front page of the *Boston Globe*."

Not everyone cared about lacrosse, of course, or about where Welles was from or what he was into. Different elements, different orbits.

Two orbits collided late on a Friday night in Duchesne East in November of Welles's freshman year. By all the obvious signs, Welles was adjusting to college life well. He liked a lot of the guys on his floor, was excited about the spring lacrosse schedule, and was handling his class load well. As for the freedoms on campus, he was starting to explore. Drinking was a pastime for the majority of BC students, and the bars in Chestnut Hill teemed with underage students carrying fake IDs most weekend nights. It was a college hobby for many, including Welles. There was no VAASA pledge to honor, and no one watching if or what he drank. In the first few months of his freshman year, he joined friends and teammates, finding his preferences and his limits.

Some classmates didn't find theirs.

On one Friday night, Welles and a few others were crowded into a dorm room on the floor, hanging out, playing video games plugged into the television, aglow in the light from the small screen. It was late, the room was loud, the door was open.

Another freshman, coming back from a night of drinking at a nearby bar, walked inside, drawn in by the gathering. Looking around, Welles was easy to mark as the smallest guy in the bunch. Even sitting down, he looked slighter, thinner, without the muscle he'd pack on to his frame through training over the next four years. The interloper was drunk, loud, and aggressive. He started to mock the video game players.

"Look at this bunch of pussies," he said.

The others looked at him. Someone suggested he go back to his room.

"Go to bed," one of his classmates said.

The suggestion went ignored. The freshman continued and, looking around the room, he seized on the smallest guy there. He started in on Welles. For whatever reason, whatever the exact gibe or the precise posture, he got physical. The drinker reached over, grabbed Welles by the shirt, and lifted him up.

That was it.

Without bothering to say anything, Welles punched him across the face, pulled him to the floor, and got on top of him. He pounded him, at one point grabbing him by the ears and bouncing his head off the dorm room's floor. He opened cuts on the other freshman's face, knocked out one of his teeth, and in the process managed to break his own hand.

Which was the reason for the phone call to Upper Nyack. It was past three A.M. Jeff answered.

"Hello," he said, only half awake.

"This is Officer Gay, I'm with the Boston College Police."

Jeff's mind rushed to every dark place a father might find in the middle of the night.

"Oh, my lord, what happened?"

"I just want to let you know," the officer said, "I'm at Saint Elizabeth's Hospital with your son, Welles."

The hospital? He's in the hospital!

"They're putting a cast on his hand," Jeff heard. "He broke his right hand."

"Oh, my God . . . how?"

"Well, apparently he was in a fight in the dorm."

Jeff asked right away, "Was alcohol involved?"

"Not your son, but the other boy, yes." Then the officer asked, "But we want to know if you want to swear out an order of protection?"

A what? Against who?

"Can I talk to Welles?"

Welles got on to explain what happened, making sure to bring his father's words back.

"Dad," he said, "this kid started the fight and you always told me, never start a fight but if someone starts with you . . ."

There was a pause.

"I finished it."

"Okay. Well, all right." And then Jeff remembered the officer's question.

"You want an order of protection?"

"Dad," Welles said, "I don't need an order of protection. That guy is going to stay the hell away from me, as far as he can."

After six semesters and three lacrosse seasons (he loved the guys, the practices, the games; a middling record and lack of championships was a whole other thing), Welles decided it was time to take a break. Not to relax, but to explore. Not on a different campus but another continent.

Welles first met Chuck Platz in the summer of 1998 in Madrid.

A business student at Quinnipiac College in Connecticut, Platz had already done a semester abroad in the city, where his family owned a small apartment, and decided to stay on through the summer, as part of an international summer program run by Syracuse University.

For Welles, the move was a more surprising one. After spending his college summers working and hanging out in Boston and Cape Cod, New York City and Nyack, fulfilling the expectations of all around him—parents, coaches, friends—the chance to break the pattern of school/sport/job was appealing, even thrilling. He'd be far from the firehouse and the lacrosse field, separated from those who already had his identity sketched and measured. It was a chance to draw a different picture and discover another self. He'd talked some about studying abroad since arriving at BC, and the Madrid program seemed the right opportunity, as a business major, to study the concepts and functions of international markets.

That was the academic mission. If there were also chances to dine on tapas and sip wine, to smoke the occasional cigar, and to experience the mysteries of Spanish women, this was all part of learning the culture.

The first time the two met was at a program reception in a hotel across the street from the university. The group was chatting in a loose circle in the lobby. Most everyone was dressed casually. Having spent the previous semester there, Platz was dressed like a typical Spaniard. "Jeans that were way too tight," he recalled, "with too many buttons."

Not Welles. He was in a navy blue Brooks Brothers suit and brown shoes, as if he were headed to a job interview or a board presentation after the reception. He was at once more formal and more forward than anyone else there.

The two hit it off immediately. They were matched up as interns, and assigned to work together at Midland Gestion, an investment bank in the city. They spent their days learning the rudiments of financial research, learning how to evaluate companies. They reported to the president, Javier Carral Martinez, who met with the two young Americans without a set schedule, and appeared to listen to them earnestly, or, at least, good-naturedly.

At night they spent time in the ancient practices of the student abroad: pondering their future paths in the States, and wondering where the next best bar stop might be.

Both shared the desire to find a job in New York City after graduating, preferably in finance. What that job would be mattered less than where. Manhattan was not the setting; it was the point.

All too soon, the program was ending.

Uncertain when they'd see each other again, Welles and Platz downplayed their parting. Platz was staying in Spain for another month, and Welles was returning to his last year in Chestnut Hill, his final season with the stick in his hand.

"I'm not really a fan of good-byes," Welles said.

It wouldn't really be good-bye, as it turned out.

For the more than eight thousand undergrads at BC there were more than a dozen on-campus housing options—limestone halls or brick-faced dorms with names like Greycliff and Vanderslice, Thayer and Walsh, befitting the school's architectural aesthetic. "The Mods" didn't have the same ring to it, nor did they deserve it.

Originally constructed as modular housing, the rectangular-sided boxes had a strange appeal despite their unsightliness. They were coveted by students wanting the off-campus house party experience while still living on campus.

In the housing lottery, they were a prized pick for seniors of all stripes, and seemed to attract certain athletes in particular, like lacrosse players, and the friends of the players, and their friends a couple of times removed.

As for what the accommodations were like inside, one resident summed it up:

"They were . . . *junky*." *Cruddy* also came up.

Six students shared the same unit in a Mod, which connected to another unit, for a total of twelve housemates. It was an unwieldy but useful number, large enough to be a force for chaos, a gathering in itself, but also a gang big enough to allow for factions and subsets. You could join in or break off, depending on your mood or agenda. If the solitary pursuit of academic transcendence was the goal, this probably wasn't the place to gain it. But if you wanted an experience that shouldn't be replicated once the degrees were conferred, you were home.

So it was for Welles and eleven others during their senior year, living in the Mods units 22A and 22B. There were Chris Gangloff and Ben Gird, Justin Patnode and Robb Aumiller, Scott Dunn, and George Leuchs. Leuchs remembered the first time Welles made a clear impression on him. After getting the housing assignment at the end of their junior year, the group had already put together eleven guys, and over the summer still needed to find a twelfth. Someone mentioned Welles, a known quantity as a lacrosse player, familiar to some in the group but not all.

Welles planned to come by the off-campus house where a few of the guys were living, to talk. He came in, a sheepish look on his face, and immediately asked a question.

"Um," he began, "does anybody own a car out front?"

The guys looked around the room. Why?

"Well, because . . ." He didn't finish the sentence. Instead, he held up a large car bumper. He'd just sheared it off trying to pull his van into the driveway.

"He was driving around this big passenger van," Leuchs recalled, "like one of those souped-up vans you drive around the country for the entire summer. It probably had a little bed in it."

The driveway next to the house was barely large enough for a small sedan. Trying to pull the van in, he miscalculated, failed to adjust in time, and in one seamless motion caught the bumper of the parked car and ripped it clean off. The aggrieved owner didn't live in the house, which perhaps explained why Welles was unanimously accepted as the twelfth member of their senior Mod.

In each unit, the six mates were split into three bedrooms. Welles bunked with Johnny Howells. They'd met as freshmen, crossing paths in dorm hallways or at parties. Howells, who'd grown up in Atlanta, was a bit of a Southern transplant, a rugby player. Not until the group formed in the Mod did any real bond grow. Quickly enough, they were friends—honest and close, needling and protective of each other.

"Just spending that much time," Howells recalled, "getting to know him day in and day out, and getting to know his family, that's when I came to appreciate him."

But . . .

"There were definitely times when . . ." He paused, and spoke in the blunt tongue of a friend. "He was annoying."

The irritation usually came from spontaneity. Welles was rarely more than a few moments away from the next idea. *Let's grab the T. Let's head into the city. Let's go to Newport. Let's get a martini at a bar downtown.* Late Sunday mornings were ripe times for these suggestions. To a hungover roommate, the proposals landed somewhere in the space between unwelcome and abhorrent.

Let's go horseback riding.

Howells rolled his eyes and put his head under the pillow. Come on, dude. Leave me alone. Welles was rarely deterred.

Looking back on some of those irritating moments years later, Howells had a different, almost doleful, view.

"He always wanted to do more," he said. "I just look back and I'm like, I shouldn't have given him a hard time."

. . .

He went out in style.

Welles's senior year.

One January night in 1999. Holiday break was over; the final semester of his college career was upon him.

The back end of that January had seen a stretch of fourteen consecutive days with higher than normal temperatures, peaking on the twenty-fourth at a balmy 62 degrees. But the stretch started after a turbulent cycle of temperature changes in the middle of the month. At one point, there was rain followed by snow followed by rain followed by a sudden 40-degree plummet across Boston and much of New England, the drop coming in a matter of hours, before the melt could be absorbed back into the saturated ground. The result that January 15 in the space around the Mods was a winter miracle.

The grassy courtyard between the buildings had completely frozen over, into a two-inch-thick sheet of ice. In one day, a perfect rink appeared outside the back door. It was a freak occurrence. It was a pedestrian danger. To a hockey player, it was an invitation.

But skating on the ice of an otherwise grassy yard was not adventure enough. To raise the stakes, Welles decided to take off his clothes, all the way down to the boxer shorts, the better to complete the scene. Out the back door he went, into a frigid midnight, gliding in easy loops and cutting crisp circles.

Howells and a few others in the unit nearly fell down laughing at the sight. They also couldn't help but wonder how far Welles would be willing to go. One opened the door and called him over. Welles, skin red, smile bright, fog blowing out of his mouth, made a sharp stop near the door. The next step was obvious.

Bet you won't take the boxers off . . .

Done. It was no easy maneuver in subfreezing temperatures to remove one's underwear while wearing blades on one's feet, but soon enough, Welles was buck naked.

Back he went into the skating routine. By this time, the entire house was in an uproar, his friends falling over one another, wondering how long he could last. Then someone realized that it was a shame to deprive anyone in the Mods the sight.

"One of the guys started playing music," Howells said, "to make more people watch." Slowly, heads started to peek out windows to investigate, and then to cheer and jeer the nude man in the hockey skates. Someone in the house flipped on the outdoor lights to improve the visibility, particularly for the women in houses across from the rink. Quickly enough, the scene was an X-rated spectacle, one man celebrating his body, in his element against the elements, stripped and flying free in the New England winter. Sober or buzzed, exhibitionist or maverick, free spirit or house jester, Welles owned the moment and the Mods, unconcerned with shrinkage or too numb to care. He had a venue and an audience, and the impulse was reason enough to risk any reaction.

After skating across the slick space, after absorbing all the taunts and shouts, after wondering if frostbite might be getting the better of the best of him, he skated over to the back of the house. There was only one problem.

"Being good roommates," Howells said, "we locked the door."

As the father is talking, his voice pauses between one story and the next, and in the space between words the slide show plays again. The picture comes without conjuring. It appears, sudden and bright.

The image of the boy, now a man, comes to him with clarity. It is a splendid Monday in spring. May 24, 1999. He is high up in the stands of Alumni Stadium, in a crowd looking over the football field at Boston College. The field is filled with students, 2,140 of them dressed in cap and gown. The class of 1999 is about to graduate, to turn its tassel and grasp its degree, to step away from the leafy campus in Chestnut Hill and into the wider world.

The problem for the father is, he can't find his son. His vantage point is perfect for taking in the entire scene, but poor for spotting a single person. All the young men and women stand so far below, a dark monolith facing away from his lens. He wants to see his son's face, and for the son to see his, to see his pride.

For such moments, when the father was in a crowd or at a distance and there was no easy way to get his son's attention, he'd developed a call the son would instantly recognize, a sound he'd respond to by instinct, no matter how loud or chaotic the circumstances. He started using the sound when his son was just a boy, playing hockey or lacrosse or football, often to celebrate a goal, or a score, or a big play. Each time, the son would look back or up or across toward the father. It became a reflex. It was their code.

If the call ever embarrassed the boy, he never let on. As he grew older, and his games became more competitive, and the sports more serious, teammates would sometimes make fun of it, or ask if he ever wanted to tell his father to stop making the sound. But the boy never told his father, and he never asked him to stop.

So, from high up in the stadium now, trying to get his son's attention, he lowers the camera. All around, other families are yelling and shouting for their graduates, trying to make the same connection, to take the same picture.

When the father signals, the sound cuts through all others like an arrow. It pierces the din, dropping into the son's ear. He hears and he turns back up to face the stands. He looks, and then delivers the smile, aimed toward the sound, and at the father, and into the lens.

What the camera can't capture is the sound—the one the father hears as the soundtrack of the slide show, the song of the code, the note that would always find its way to his son's ear.

It is the sound of a siren.

C all it a very long pass, across fourteen years, from one lacrosse player to another. That's how Welles landed the job so many others coveted. He was headed to Wall Street.

The foot into Sandler O'Neill, a small but powerful investment banking firm specializing in the financial sector, came from a hometown connection, Stacey Sennas McGowan, a managing director at Sandler. She was the president of her class all four years at Nyack High School, and after graduating in 1981, she went on to play varsity lacrosse as a team captain at Boston College. During Welles's sophomore year, he and Alison had talked about what he planned to do the upcoming summer. He was interested in finance, so Alison had a conversation with Fran Sennas, Stacey's mother, and shortly thereafter, Welles was on his way to apply for an internship.

At the interview, Welles was asked, "What would you say if I told you we weren't going to pay you anything this summer?"

"That's okay," he said. "The experience will really be worth it."

"Of course we are going to pay you," the interviewer said. "But I like your attitude."

He was in. Five days a week. Eight weeks. His summer of work. Each day he drove over the Tappan Zee Bridge to Tarrytown with Jeff. Together, they took the train to Grand Central Terminal, and from there, Welles caught the subway downtown. He liked it immediately, all of it: the firm was filled with characters, the city a throbbing buzz. The weeks flew by, and he made a good impression. Two years later, Welles was back, hired as a junior associate. He started almost immediately after graduation.

The job wasn't exactly *on* Wall Street. The offices were roughly a quarter mile northwest of it. He could see them anytime he wanted to from the apartment he found, with a few college classmates, across the river in Hoboken, New Jersey. He was working at 2 World Trade Center. Twenty-two years old with a view to forever, or at least the sliver of forever glimpsed from the tower's windows, pinched between protruding columns on either side.

The South Tower. The 104th floor.

T he dress code for the office was unwritten. There was no line in an employee handbook, or direct mention during orientation. There didn't have to be. The fashion template was simple and inflexible. Casual Fridays were for insurance offices and weak enterprises that had lost their edge. This was finance, son. Wear a suit.

And Welles did, happily. It was part of the identity he sought in working at Sandler, going back to the summer internship. Most of his suits were regular Brooks Brothers issue, different hues of blue and gray, with a crisp white or blue shirt and the accompanying yellow, red, or blue tie.

Very early in his tenure there, during the autumn of 1999, Welles chose to accessorize a bit, and in doing so made one of his first discoveries in professional life, even when it came to the benign field of wardrobe. He learned a fast lesson.

"There was a period of time where the guys would be wearing suspenders," Jimmy Dunne, Sandler's senior managing principal, recalled. "I did it for a while."

As one of the firm's founding partners, Dunne could wear whatever he wanted.

It was another matter for a junior associate, who had barely cashed his first few paychecks, to wear the braces. Not that Welles understood the distinction, until the first time a senior associate saw him working in equity research with his suit jacket off. Whether the suspenders were plain or cartoonish didn't matter. There was a rule, unwritten or not, and Welles had broken it.

The senior trader came up behind Welles and, without warning, pulled the suspenders sharply back and then released them, slapping his back with a loud and painful snap.

"Who the hell do you think you are, J. P. Morgan?" he asked.

Welles looked at him, confused.

"After you make a million dollars here, then maybe you can wear suspenders. Until then, don't ever wear those things again." The trader walked away, laughing.

But there was one part of Welles's personal dress code that would not be subject to office fashion or bent to anyone's unwritten rule. It was a constant, tucked in the back right pocket of every set of trousers and every pair of suit pants he wore every day. There were times when he would take it out, place it on his desk, and leave it there, though few noticed.

Natalie McIver did.

The assistant to the director of equity research at Sandler, she spent a lot of time with the firm's junior associates. Research was typically the first posting for those just joining the company.

Many of the junior associates wanted to leave research quickly after a relatively short tour of three or four months. They wanted to move to the rush of the trading desk, or the rewards of fixed income, or the prestige of mergers and acquisitions, whether with Sandler or not. To those new to Wall Street, the trading desks were the bright precincts where fortunes were made and the path to rooms where deals were forged. For the uninitiated, research, though essential, could feel like time in the salt mines, back of the house.

McIver sensed that Welles was different. While he might not be destined for a career as a research analyst, he didn't have the air of a man passing through or biding his time. The work was demanding, and that suited Welles just fine.

He was at his desk each day before eight, and stayed as late as the day demanded. During earnings season, it demanded quite a lot.

"The quarterly earnings for all the stocks that we covered, that becomes like a reporting frenzy," McIver said. Often, multiple companies reported their earnings on the same day. "That would go on for almost one month per quarter," she said. "So that was four times a year where it was like a month, solid, of crunch time."

The hours were often long and stressful, but Welles showed little wear. Even in the busiest weeks, he kept his sense of wonder about where he worked, at the nerve center of the financial world, 1,126 feet up in the sky.

During one of the busier weeks, with everyone in the department juggling multiple reports and assignments, McIver was surprised by a tap on her shoulder and a sudden introduction.

"Natalie," Welles said, "this is my dad."

He'd given no notice that his father would be visiting, or that he would be taking time out of the day to show Jeff around the office. "None of us ever did that," she said. "Nobody ever brought their family through that I'd remembered. It was just so neat that he didn't take it for granted. I would meet my dad for lunch, but he would meet me downstairs. I never brought him around. I never thought of bringing him up."

McIver watched as Welles guided his father through the office. The visit was short, but Welles made sure to show off the star attraction: the view from the narrow windows westward, where the research department faced, looking out over the Hudson and Jersey City, where she lived, and beyond.

What struck McIver too was Welles's ability to keep the job in perspective. His father's visit was one example; another was the red bandanna in his back pocket.

The first time she noticed it, Welles had taken it out and placed it on his desk. This was easy fodder, and the response was quick.

"What are you doing with *that*?" she asked. "I'm the one from Ohio. What are you doing carrying a bandanna?"

It became a source of ribbing and jabbing whenever Welles took it out. McIver and another research associate, Judd Cavalier, led the charge.

"What are you, a cowboy?"

"You forget this is New York? This isn't the South!"

"Howdy do there, Welles?"

Welles would laugh and offer his own jabs right back, but the bandanna remained, either in his pocket or on his desk.

Most people in the office had no idea he carried it, or what its origins were. But those like McIver, who worked close to him in those first few months at Sandler, as he was just beginning to build a career and discover what life might be like looking at a computer screen, days spent wearing a suit and answering a deadline and earning a salary, recalled it clearly.

Whenever someone needed something extra done, some deadline beaten, some thorny issue solved, the response was predictable.

"We would always tease him," she said. "Someone would just say, 'Hey, Welles, can you do . . . ?' Anything. Fill in the blank. 'Hey, you've got to solve this, fix this trade report . . .'"

In a dramatic gesture, Welles would reach for the bandanna on his desk or in his pocket, lift it above his head, and wave it in the air.

"He would say, 'This is where the magic comes from,'" McIver recalled.

Other times—"I'm a superhero."

And once, facing some tall task, he lifted the bandanna, stood up from his chair, and made a preposterous declaration that McIver never forgot.

"I'm going to save the world."

You've got to come up and see the office."

For Johnny Howells, the request was hardly a surprise. Knowing Welles since their freshman year at Boston College, living with him in the Mods in their senior year, Howells had grown used to spur-of-the-moment ideas. Howells was visiting from Massachusetts. He liked coming to see his buddies who'd relocated to the city, or as close as their paychecks could afford. For Welles, it was a shared basement apartment in Hoboken, a short train ride away.

It was a Sunday, and for most newly graduated from the soft schedule of college life to the grind of earning a living, the office was barely tolerable five days a week, if at all. Welles was already working more than fifty, even sixty, hours at Sandler O'Neill during the busiest times, and the weekends should've been a necessary relief, if not a complete disconnect. His love for the city, and for the office address in particular, was a magnet for him, though, especially with a friend in town. But Howells also sensed a slight detachment as well. He liked that shade of dispassion; he saw in it a measure of humility.

"I don't know everybody that works on Wall Street," Howells said. "But they think they're very important, and they're doing important work, and I never got that feeling about Welles. He wanted to make a good living, he wanted to live in the area, and why not?"

But for Welles to become the suit he was wearing five days a week? His career was just starting, really, not even a year old. Still, Howells didn't see it.

Taking the train beneath the Hudson, the two friends made their way to Lower Manhattan and Chambers Street. Without the press of commuters and clamor of the workweek, the atmosphere around the entire World Trade Center complex felt oddly still, as if on pause. The two entered the lobby of 2 World Trade, and then took the elevator ride and transfer on the 78th floor before finally reaching the 104th floor of the South Tower.

Sandler's offices were deserted. The view was, of course, the reason to come, and together they absorbed the panorama through the narrow windows, the city's full scale laid out like a map beneath them. The sunny day's brilliance surrounded them on all sides. It was beautiful.

Welles took Howells over to his area of the office, in research. His cubicle was perhaps ten feet from a window overlooking the East River, facing away from his apartment and New Jersey.

"Hey," he said, "take a look at this." He took out a glass from his desk, poured water into it, and placed it down on a flat surface. As winds hit the building, Howells saw the water tremble and move, caught in the building's natural sway. Welles showed him how some of the office doors swayed slightly on their hinges as the building registered its gentle tremors. The structure was a living thing, beneath and around them, and Howells could see the spell it cast on his friend, the pride he took in displaying its quirks of personality. This is why he wanted to make the trip. Not once during the tour could Howells remember him talking about the research, the reports, the job.

"I didn't get the impression that he was infatuated with what he was doing," Howells said, "as much as where he was."

. . .

I t was a surprising offer.

Welles and Chuck Platz, his friend from the summer in Madrid, had spoken only a handful of times since they'd returned to the States, keeping vague tabs on each other's movements. There was little to prepare Platz for the moment the phone rang.

"Hey," Welles said, as if they'd spent every other weekend hanging out. "Want to be roommates?"

It was the spring of 2000, and Welles was ready to move from Hoboken, to graduate fully into the life he wanted, and was seeking someone to join him, someone who had the same taste for city life that he did. Platz was living with his aunt and uncle in Westchester, trying to save money, making the commute to his job at an asset management firm based on Park Avenue. He was wandering the aisles in a local Staples when Welles rang. The timing was perfect. The answer was easy. Sure. Sounds great. Have you found a place yet? Minor detail.

Welles and Platz got a place fast, almost as soon as they started the search in earnest. They visited a spot in the West Village, just the second apartment they considered. Welles arrived first, checked it out, and headed back downstairs. Before Platz even got inside for his own look, he saw Welles walking down the street toward him, taking big strides, a huge smile on his face. Platz knew.

"Just seeing him," he said, "I said to myself, 'This is where we're going to live.'"

They knew the rent would be hard, but not insurmountable. Few things are for young people eager to wade into city life, drawn by the undertow of its wonder and chance. For a rooftop look south at the towers, for a two-bedroom with an honest-togoodness eat-in kitchen and space for an aquarium, the lease terms were a happy ransom. It would be worth every cent.

The apartment offered a view—if you stood next to the toilet, leaned hard against the wall, craned your neck upward out the top third of the bathroom window, and kept your balance, you might see it: a sliver of the upper reaches of the Empire State Building. That was north.

The view south was just slightly less limiting, but through one of the bedroom windows, at just the right angle, you could see the peaks of two silver streams reaching skyward. A trip out the apartment door, down the hallway, and up two flights of stairs to the roof of the building took them to a far more inspiring view. A mile south of the rooftop, piercing the horizon, drawing every eye: the soaring towers of the World Trade Center.

Not that Welles or Platz made the trip to the roof daily, or even weekly. They were busy, immersed in the daily lives of young professionals in the city, outwardly aspiring masters of the universe, and inwardly wandering through the hollows of that aspiration. But they never lost the feeling that they had scored: 115 Washington Place, prewar, downtown, two bedrooms, on the fifth floor, a mile from work. The rent was $2,500 a month. Bite down, suck it up, move on in.

For Welles, it felt destined. The apartment number was 19— his lucky number for as long as anyone could remember, the digits he wore on every jersey from the time he was a boy, the number he wore through his lacrosse career at Boston College. The figure was his talisman.

They loaded in on September 15, 2000.

"It was a stretch," Platz said. "We were both young in our ca-

reers, so it took two of the four paychecks we got a month to pay the rent. But to this day, I would rent that place again in a heart-beat.

If not for the memory."

Long days. Short years.

Time passed quickly outside the walls of apartment 19. The two men kept similar schedules, but with enough separation for each to have time in the pad by himself when he needed it, which wasn't often. Typically Welles left for his day before Platz did, and returned home first. Welles headed south in horizontal terms and then dramatically north vertically, to his spot on the 104th floor at Sandler. Platz was more earthbound, going north-east to his office in Midtown, in the Grace Building, across Forty-second Street from Bryant Park. A few times a week after work, they made sure to meet at any number of city watering holes, typically back in the Village. A favorite was Boxers on West Fourth Street, a reliable bar and grill with cold beer and thick burgers, since closed, where they basked in their status as regulars.

During many of the weeknights out, they reminisced about their summer days together in Madrid, and wondered if there might be a financially constructive way to relive them—by creating a business that connected them to Spain. While they weren't exactly sure what services they might provide, or who their clients would be, or how such an idea would yield profits, they did have a name: Iberian Ventures. It would be a consulting firm, to identify and connect countries ready to benefit from a trading relationship. There was a simpler motive as well.

"We thought of it as an opportunity for us to get back there," Platz said.

While they chewed on the idea fitfully over the months, often at Boxers, Welles also brought up another job, a much more radical departure from Sandler. Half a dozen times, at least, into the spring and summer of 2001, he raised the idea with Platz, working it out in his mind, trying to speak it into existence.

"I'm thinking of taking the test," Welles said. "Taking the exam."

Platz would look at his roommate and smile.

He understood how deeply rooted the notion was, reaching back to boyhood. Welles wasn't talking about the GRE or LSAT, some standardized assessment for graduate school.

No.

"It was the exam," Platz said, "to become a New York City fireman."

This is a picture that never plays in the father's slide show. In hindsight, it is too fraught. In the frame, Welles stands next to an old family friend, Harry Wanamaker Jr., two men in an easy pose beside each other, both strong and smiling, one older and one younger, one in uniform, the other in a polo shirt. They have known each other a long time.

There is a story that the older man's family would tell about him decades after it happened. On a day when Harry Wanamaker Jr. was being celebrated for many official acts of valor, they related an episode that took place on a vacation. Wanamaker spent his life in Upper Nyack, but he and his family enjoyed time away on Cape Cod during the summer. On one of those trips, after the family had spent the evening at a local amusement park, Wanamaker looked up to see smoke drifting through the air, floating high above the trees into the night. He instantly knew it wasn't exhaust from a generator or smoke from a grill at the park. His training told him as much.

Together with his wife and children, Wanamaker got in his car and traced the direction of the smoke back to its source. A nearby house was on fire, flame and smoke pouring from the second floor. There were neighbors on the home's lawn, screaming that sometimes kids were left at the house; they were uncertain if anyone was still inside.

No trucks or local firefighters were on the scene yet.

"Dad jumped out of the car and ran into the house wearing only shorts and a T-shirt," his daughter Gail recalled. "We were little kids and watched from the car and held our breath," she said. "Thankfully, no one was in the house, but the five minutes Dad was inside with no gear was intense for us. It was the first time we really had seen him in action. It opened us up to what he did every day that he went to work."

It was a life's work for Wanamaker. After graduating from Nyack High School in 1961, and then serving in the navy, he returned home to become a Nyack police officer, and spent time as a lineman for a local utility company. He worked hard, but those posts were merely placeholders as he waited for the call he wanted most. He got it in 1968, when the Fire Department of New York accepted his application. At twenty-five years old, he was a city firefighter.

He would serve the department for the next thirty-seven years in some of the busiest fire stations across the five boroughs, including tours in Harlem and the South Bronx. In 1982, he rose to the rank of lieutenant. In all, he'd earn six Certificates of Merit, for various acts of bravery, and received the Columbia Association Medal for valor on the steps of City Hall. For all the calls he answered at all the different stations, with the "Bronx Bombers of Ladder 49," or the decade spent with Engine 92, his appetite for fighting fires never faded. To satisfy that passion, and to pass on the lessons he'd learned at his day job, he did it in his free time as well, volunteering at his local fire department, Empire Hook and Ladder Company No. 1 in Upper Nyack.

Wanamaker spent nearly fifty years in the old brick firehouse on North Broadway in every conceivable role, helping any way he could. At times, it was the most direct way, putting down residential and commercial fires as part of the company's response to alarms. At others, it was teaching. The newest to join the department, regardless of age, regarded him with awe.

In his time at Empire, seven members of Empire Hook and Ladder, including Wanamaker's cousin Paul, followed his path into the FDNY.

Wanamaker took great pride in that, and in training the volunteers at Empire, most of whom would never join New York's bravest. Of those, he had a special place in his heart for Welles, whom he first knew as the young boy who would tag along with his father, crawling into the tightest spaces of the company's trucks, where grown men could never fit, and didn't want to try. Headfirst, he'd nearly disappear to clean some distant nook. Whether it needed cleaning was less important than what he gained upon crawling out—the feeling that he'd pleased his father, that he'd contributed, and that one day he would belong to the company and be called on to help, the same way the veterans were.

It was Wanamaker, among others, who worked with Welles as a junior member of the department at sixteen years old.

Six years later, Lt. Harry Wanamaker Jr. was fifty-eight, a veteran of the department who had earned a plum assignment with Marine Company 1, New York City's first marine fire brigade. And upon the deck of Marine 1's big boat years later, he'd pose beside Welles on an early summer night.

Marine 1 consisted of two boats, actually, with the larger vessel considered the standard-bearer of the department's fleet. The fireboat's formal name was the *John D. McKean,* 334 gross tons heavy, 129 feet long, and more than forty years old. She was a steady warhorse, with two 1,000-horsepower propulsion engines and a fuel capacity of 7,000 gallons, enough to operate for more than four days before running dry. The *McKean* looked like a little boy's vision of a fireboat, from her red-and-white color scheme to her wide and squat smokestack to the enormous brass water cannon on her nose. When called into action, she was capable of pumping 19,000 gallons of water per minute.

She was also perfect for an evening cruise, as she was doing in June 2001, with Wanamaker as host. The group knew Wanamaker well and jumped at his invitation. His guests had driven down from the Hudson Valley in Rockland County to meet him along the water on the west side of Lower Manhattan. Wanamaker had cleared the group, a handful of volunteer firefighters, for a short tour. The guests were from Empire Hook and Ladder Company No. 1 and other members of the Nyack Fire Department. Welles and his father were among the first to climb aboard.

"It was a beautiful evening," Jeff Crowther said. "We took some sandwiches and sodas and cruised around the harbor, around the Statue of Liberty, and back up the East River. We had a lovely time."

As the light started to fade, the volunteers took in the unparalleled vistas of the city at sunset seen from the water, the glowing Battery at the southern tip of the island, and the blaze of Midtown, the gray corridors of buildings slipping by.

At one point, Jeff wondered where Welles was. He hadn't seen him in a while, and wanted them to appreciate the city's twilight together, but his son was nowhere in sight.

"I didn't see Welles for about an hour and then he popped up. I said, 'Hey, where you been?'"

"I was talking with one of the firefighters," Welles said.

"For an hour?" Jeff asked.

Welles just smiled and looked out at the Hudson's dark mercury and beyond, to the city shimmering in the fading light. He was enthralled by the moment: the setting, the camaraderie, and the conversation he'd just had with Tommy Sullivan, one of Marine 1's crew.

Sullivan was ten years older than Welles but looked young for thirty-four, with thick black hair and a strong build. From the time he was a boy, water was in his blood. His first experiences on the river were working as a teenager in Stony Point, New York, scraping barnacles off boats. After a stint with the NYPD, he moved over to the fire department in the mid-1990s, an uncommon move. He'd been with the department for seven years.

Less than a decade later, Sullivan would play a heroic role in one of the greatest moments in the history of Marine 1, and one of the proudest for the FDNY. On the freezing afternoon of January 15, 2009, US Airways Flight 1549 came down for an emergency landing on the Hudson after both of its engines failed. Getting the call in their firehouse on the pier, Marine 1's crew instantly divided. Five crew members were aboard the *John D. McKean,* the proper fireboat, while Sullivan and two crewmates raced out on Marine 1's *Alpha,* a twenty-seven-foot fast-response boat, moving north at forty-five miles per hour. Minutes later, Sullivan was throwing life preservers into the water and lifting passengers off the partially submerged left wing of the plane and onto the deck of the *Alpha.*

One of the women he rescued, forty-seven-year-old Beverly Waters, told the *New York Times,* "He pulled me up like it was nothing for him."

Considered the most successful ditching of a commercial jet in history, the rescue of all 155 passengers and crew aboard the flight was dubbed "The Miracle on the Hudson" and made a national star out of its pilot, Captain Chesley "Sully" Sullenberger. Local commercial vessels from the NY Waterway company played a vital role in the safe evacuations, as did boats from the coast guard, NYPD, and FDNY. On that frigid day, Sullivan's boat, which had a maximum capacity of sixteen including crew, carried twenty rescued passengers to a triage center for medical treatment. For its part in the episode, the city's fire department fleet received renewed attention and respect, and, in time, more resources for water rescues.

But all that lay in the future that evening. Nothing more was written across the water than its own slow currents. That Welles would have the chat with Sullivan was no surprise. He was endlessly curious, a natural conversation starter, and he already knew plenty of city firefighters from Empire Hook and Ladder, including Wanamaker. What was unusual was that he didn't tell his father about what they'd discussed, at least not then.

Years later, Sullivan remembered meeting Welles and Jeff, but the precise details of the conversation had faded. He knew both were volunteers at Empire and friends of Harry's, and recalled spending time with Welles and liking him. He surmised what he would have said when Welles asked his inevitable question about life with the FDNY.

What's it really like? How do you like it?

"I would've told him," Sullivan said, "that I loved it."

Sullivan loved the teamwork and camaraderie so much that he regularly showed up early for his twenty-four-hour shift, and many days stayed late after his replacement arrived. He was where he wanted to be, doing what mattered to him. It was the life he loved. There was no other purpose to match it, not the rush of the calls or the challenge of the rescues or the clarity of the mission. To serve.

As the boat coasted down the Hudson toward its home berth,

Jeff, Welles, and Wanamaker ended up side by side on the top deck.

"Welles," Jeff said. "Let me get a picture of you and Harry."

Jeff lifted the camera toward them as they moved together, shoulder to shoulder, Harry in his light blue uniform shirt with a black sash and radio handset across his chest. Welles stood beside him. As Jeff prepared to take the picture before any more light leaked away, Welles stopped him. He wanted to be sure the setting was just right.

"Dad," he said, "make sure you get the Twin Towers in the background."

Jeff paused, years later, thinking back to that June night in 2001. Without having to hold it in his hands, he saw the image before him. "You can clearly see the World Trade Center towers off to the right of where they were standing."

The buildings top the skyline on the left side of the picture, reaching into darkness.

. . .

A few months later, in early August, Welles made a call home. The city was in the midst of a stifling stretch of summer heat and humidity, with temperatures in Central Park peaking at 104, baking the air. It was the kind of weather that felt like breathing in carsickness with every step out the door. For anyone unable to escape to the Jersey shore or to the beaches on Long Island, the city was a hotbox.

Welles wasn't calling his father to talk about the weather. There was a restlessness on his end of the line, a sense that while the shirts he'd worn for the past few years still fit him, the collars were growing tighter and beginning to chafe.

After some small talk, Welles got to the point.

"Dad," he said, with a slight pause, "I think I want to change my career."

"Excuse me?" came the instant reply.

Welles had made the hard and prized move to Sandler's trading desk a few months before. He'd been with the company more than a year and a half, and now was in position to begin reaping serious rewards. For an equities trader at Sandler in the furious cycle of buying and selling, each day came with a scoreboard attached, based on the market's closing numbers. It was intense work, exhilarating at times, but exacting always; you didn't lightly step away from the game before the market closed and the scoreboard issued its tally.

Welles heard the note of incredulity in his father's voice. He expected it.

Jeff Crowther had spent his entire career in banking. He had many passions, to be sure, many of which he shared with his son. But a sound and secure profession came first, a career like the one Welles was beginning to build at Sandler. And it was a good career, as far as Jeff understood it. Welles had already shown the ability to grow and be recognized. He'd made the leap from research to the trading desk, a precinct that carried with it the real possibility of making a fortune. Not a faraway dream of striking it rich. Not standing in line for a golden ticket. Not drilling down into some patch of Texas dust, or toiling in some Silicon Valley garage. Sandler was a Wall Street finance player, and if one could withstand its pressures and endure its swings, there might well be a path to a lot of money. In years to come, six- and seven-figure bonuses and a bursting portfolio of his own. It was a chance at lasting, life-changing wealth.

Change his career?

Excuse me?

"I think I want to be a New York City firefighter."

There it was. He said it. Aloud. To his father. For so many of us, change first begins by giving it voice. Say it so that it might become real. Welles had just done that.

Perhaps his biggest surprise was the lack of astonishment at the other end of the line. Jeff's mind immediately turned back to the June night with Marine 1, to Welles's disappearance for an hour, to his conversation with firefighter Tommy Sullivan.

"Oh," Jeff said. "So you think you're going to get assigned to the fireboat?"

Maybe Jeff had seen the trail in the water better than Welles had assumed.

"I know it'd be cool," Jeff said. "But, you know, your dad's not some retired battalion chief from the New York City Fire Department. That's not going to help you."

It was an easy response, based on an older man's understanding of the way the world works, the connections that pave its opportunities. It was a connection from Stacey Sennas McGowan, after all, that helped Welles get his Sandler job in the first place. But Welles had already gone past the surface of the water, the superficial allure, in his mind. He'd thought about this.

"No, no, Dad," Welles said. "I understand that."

"It's going to be four or five years, at least, before you could get picked up into the fire department," Jeff countered.

"I understand that too," Welles said. And then he outlined the most basic steps he'd have to take. Not the bureaucratic or logistical ones. Those were easier, set, laid out for any applicant. He talked about the salary repercussions, the discipline he'd need. He'd calculated how to finance the move—not in the gauzy terms of a dream, but in the numbers that would support a life.

"I figure I'll just keep working here," Welles said. "I'll save all my bonuses, and save as much money as I can, and then if I join the department, if I want to get married, I'll have a nice nest egg, I can buy a house."

He'd also pondered the time it would take him to reach the department.

"I'll keep going to the gym," he said. "You know I'll keep myself in good shape. I'll still be under thirty."

Jeff listened as Welles added one more point emphatically.

"Dad, if I sit in front of this computer for the rest of my life," he said, "I'll go crazy."

. . .

When did you stop?

When did you put the hope away, shifting it from something real to something . . . lesser? As the beach house forever not built, the grand trip always postponed, the pursuit never begun? When did the dream leave you as an aspiration and float off into the province of the never-to-be? Never to be the first-round draft pick or the perennial all-star, the name above the title or the founder of the company?

Probably, *never* crept up gradually. No sudden awakening in a cold sweat, no precise moment of terrible clarity. There is often no sharp edge to surrender, no bright line between chasing and letting go of the dream of what our lives could become before we get caught in the gears of daily living, the hundreds and thousands of tiny compromises that move us through the day. The clock doesn't stop to mark the time between the last thought when your goal was still calling to you and the next, by which it had drifted past range, caught between radio stations like static, until the fade is complete. Silence.

It's a creeping capitulation, the recognition of what we're able to manage. That awareness comes in slow degrees, and at different times, in all our lives. It comes through the circumstances that shape us, the weather inside us, the failures that drag us below a line. You know the line—the one between what we want and what we accept.

Welles wasn't ready to cross that line, not entirely. Almost any time of any day, he could still look down to the street and see a flashing red dot and hear the delayed and distant echo of a siren.

The sound and vision of his dream was still answering, moving, calling.

I n the financial capital of the planet, working in finance meant a special place on earth, and held the rewards to prove it. Sandler O'Neill was a burgeoning force, and didn't attract or indulge the pale or hesitant. Its culture celebrated competition in every way, against rival firms and within its walls. The firm was filled with athletes, some not as accomplished as Welles and others more so—all of whom had grown up as inherent strivers, and winners.

There was also a natural and useful selfishness cultivated to drive the firm forward, a tapping of the capitalist vein, but, hopefully, not the whole of its heart. The principals of the firm wanted all there to master the work, but also to enjoy and appreciate it. The hours were too long, the demands too great, the expectations too high, for anyone to fake his way through. There had to be a large, if not total, buy-in to thrive.

Anyone giving less would've been perceived as lacking, when pitted against his colleagues, and was unlikely to last. The hedging would be obvious.

That's certainly what Jimmy Dunne believed. Despite his place in the firm as one of its founders, he was close to its entire staff, challenging and cultivating, nurturing and exacting. His office was close to where Welles spent much of his time on the trading desk. Dunne took pride in demanding a deep level of commitment, and in detecting when it wasn't there. He had no doubts whatsoever regarding Welles's passion for what he was doing, his investment in succeeding.

To sharpen his eye, Dunne had a pattern of questioning he followed when interviewing new graduates and new associates hoping to join or move up at Sandler. He would exchange greetings and pleasantries, easing his way in. Then he'd look across at the prospect and ask about an experience not listed on the résumé.

"So," Dunne would say, "tell me about some job, or jobs, that you really hated."

Typically, the applicant would pause and consider where this was headed, and what Dunne wanted to hear. He waited the applicant out until he got an answer—a specific one, with the name of the business and former boss, and the description of the work.

"That's where I call to check references," he said. "That way, I can find out. I want to see how the person behaves when he's doing something he doesn't quite want to do. Can he suck it up? Can he do the right thing?"

Looking back on it months later, after talking with Jeff, Dunne was caught off guard to learn that Welles had been sucking it up right in front of his boss's eyes. He'd performed the tasks before him well, even exceeded expectations, but his heart wasn't completely in the work; he wasn't fulfilled, even after the move to the trading desk. Everything about Welles from the moment he arrived signaled to Dunne a young man thriving and fully engaged. A key strength of Dunne's success, and the firm's, lay in reading people, not just markets. He took pride in it. With Welles, a young man he liked and respected, his eye missed any trace of restlessness.

"I was just shocked," Dunne said, "which was even more impressive. Because it's one thing to do something you love and do everything you can, and try to be impressive every moment, to develop sort of an indispensable nature to yourself.

"It's a very different thing if you're not sure this is what you want to do, or, worse than that, you're fairly sure this is *not* what you want to do."

Welles wanted to do something else.

Shortly after talking with his father in August, he began to explore the requirements for the FDNY.

The first was obvious. An application.

R *udy.*

That's who came to mind when Angelo Mangia met Welles shortly after the firm's newest junior associate arrived at Sandler O'Neill. It likely wasn't a description Welles would've considered flattery.

Daniel Ruettiger was the "Rudy" to whom Mangia referred, the blue-collar son depicted in the beloved 1993 sports film of the same name. The movie tells the story of an undersized but scrappy kid who dreams of playing football at Notre Dame but lacks the athletic talent and the grades to dress for the storied Fighting Irish. Ultimately, he overcomes a series of obstacles (near poverty, dyslexia, meager physical gifts) to reach his triumphant moment— suiting up for the team, playing in a game, and getting carried off the field.

Welles was, by any measure, a much better athlete and a bigger physical specimen than Rudy; he'd grown to five ten or five eleven and filled out to 180 pounds by the time he left BC. He was a better student than Rudy too. But for Mangia, that wasn't the point. The managing director drew the comparison because he saw a bit of the underdog in the new associate, and sensed the same heart. "He wasn't the biggest guy," Mangia recalled. "He wasn't the loudest guy. He was just somebody thrilled to be a part of the team, who didn't shy away from anything."

As part of Sandler's culture, the more senior members of the staff were encouraged to act as mentors to those just arriving, to make certain they felt a part of the whole, and to nurture their talent in a way that would serve the company and the individual. Mangia, an attorney who helped to handle legal matters, relished the role, the chance to be a big brother to some of the fresh faces. It fit his vision of what a workplace like Sandler's—and its associates—should be: a competitive and boisterous family driven to be profitable, of course, but also joined in their pursuits, and judged by more than reviews and bonuses. They should care about one another.

Almost from the moment Welles walked through the doors on the 104th floor to begin a Wall Street career, he landed on Mangia's radar, and the two hit it off. Why, exactly, was hard for him to pinpoint. Mangia was almost twenty years older, worked in a different area of the company, and was in a different stage of his life. He was also frustrated almost daily by the numbing commute from his home on Long Island to Lower Manhattan. Welles, living in the West Village, was largely immune to traffic snarls. His short subway ride or brisk walk home made Mangia envious.

The two did share a love for the city's excitement, its events and restaurants, its juice and edge. In Welles, Mangia saw some shades of a younger self, and enjoyed being near that reflection—drawing off a young man's energy and guiding him through the beginnings of corporate life. There were dinners and ball games, inside jokes and late nights out. They quickly grew to be friends.

As Welles made his way from the research to the trading side, Mangia could look out of his office and find his would-be protégé just fifty feet away, at his desk, energized by the bedlam and frenzy.

"There's action going on," Mangia said. "I look over and in the midst of chaos, there's Welles, and he's just beaming. Always. He's thrilled. . . . He just really loved being at the firm and you could see it."

By the spring of 2001, Mangia's own time at the firm was ending, by his choice. After one more maddening slog from the suburbs to the Financial District, he returned a call from a client, who encouraged him for months to leave Sandler. The client asked him to venture out and join another shop. The company was Standard Funding, based in Woodbury, on Long Island, nearer to his home.

Like many others at the company, Mangia didn't think he'd ever leave Sandler O'Neill. The money was too good, the rush too sweet, and he'd proved he could answer its demands. His plan was to retire there, in his time and on his terms. But the call to the client started a conversation, and soon, a new direction. He told the firm he would be leaving in May.

As his exit approached, he and Welles decided to celebrate with a dinner together. Starting off at The Red Cat, an eclectic American place on Tenth Avenue in Chelsea, they ended up making their way south for a nightcap in the Village. At a table outside a French restaurant, Welles suddenly stood up.

"Wait here," he told Mangia. "I have to go to my apartment. I'll be right back."

Before Mangia could reply, Welles was gone, without any hint of an explanation, not that his friend was altogether surprised. Welles was prone to bursts of spontaneity.

"About ten minutes later, he comes back with a bottle of champagne," Mangia said. Welles had run home to his apartment on Washington Place and back, a few city blocks away. And although there were several champagnes on the menu, he wanted to give a toast from a bottle of his own. He received the bubbles as a Christmas gift the year before from someone at the firm, and was saving it for a special occasion. A friend's departure fit the bill.

"Here," he said, popping it open. "We're going to celebrate." And so they did. Mangia couldn't see if it was Dom Pérignon or Martini & Rossi as Welles poured, and he didn't care.

Shortly after that night, Mangia packed up his office, said his good-byes, and left the Twin Towers behind to begin his new position at Standard. He said he wasn't going to be far away. He'd keep in touch. In the months that followed, he did, with several of his former colleagues at Sandler, including Welles. The two talked on the phone and exchanged e-mails regularly. "I would talk to Welles about how things were going at the firm," Mangia said. Mangia liked his new position in Woodbury, and seeing room for a young talent, he offered him a soft invitation, to see whether Welles might have an interest in doing something else.

"But that wasn't for Welles, not coming out into the suburbs."

When they spoke, he heard something in Welles's voice. But it wasn't obvious or loud, not a complaint. Mangia didn't think that was Welles's nature. Still, he heard a note not as bright, and it was a recurring theme.

"It was strange," Mangia said. "I would say, in at least four of the conversations we had over the course of that summer, he would repeat the same thing to me."

Welles told Mangia: "I don't know where I'm going to be. I just know I'm going to be part of something big."

The phrase still echoed for his friend, the voice lingering years later. "He would say that, and I would laugh, and he would laugh, and that was it."

As summer faded and Labor Day passed, Mangia checked in with Welles to ask how he was faring. He sent an e-mail. The note was simple, a reflexive inquiry between friends. "How are you doing? Hope all is well."

The answer back struck Mangia. Their e-mail exchanges were common office stuff, hardly meant to be preserved. But Mangia kept the reply. He still keeps it, printed out, in a box in his office.

The e-mail was little more than a fragment. "I'm okay, but a few words come to mind," Welles wrote. He listed the words in a terse column down the page:

Anxious. Frustrated. Aimless. Bored. Lobster. Cold beer. The coast of Maine.

Forever. Welles. Out.

"It was just very much out of character for him," Mangia said. "The words *anxious* and *Welles,* those were two words I would never use in the same sentence. You never saw him anxious. He didn't have that quality anywhere. Ever. So that gave me an uneasy feeling . . ."

Perhaps it was the feeling that kept Mangia from deleting the note instantly, as he'd often do. In time, he would print it, and ponder it. He would look at it, his eyes stopping for a moment on the date, even though he already knew. Friday, September 7, 2001.

"That was our last communication."

```
Subj: well...
Date: Fri, 7 Sep 2001 3:00:56 PM Eastern Daylight Time
From: "Welles Crowther" <wrcrowther@hotmail.com>
To:   ajmangial@aol.com

I'm okay, but a few words come to mind...
anxious
frustrated
aimless
bored
lobster
cold beer
the coast of maine
forever
welles
out
```

A weekend night for Welles shimmered with a heady mix of chance and mystery. For this big night out, September 9, 2001, Welles was in the Village with Mom and Dad alongside. Welles saw Jeff and Alison frequently, by his invitation. By the measure of most twentysomething single men working in finance, living in an apartment in Greenwich Village, he was astoundingly open with his mother and father and eager to see them whenever he could. Sure, there were boundaries, but they were the same ones his parents wanted—the proofs of independence, and the lines drawn by the differences in age and responsibility.

As a warm and dry day faded into evening in Manhattan, there was nothing to signal the night as particularly special or different. Jeff and Alison had made their way from Upper Nyack to have dinner with Welles and a few friends. Once dinner was finished, they would part ways.

It was only in hindsight that the night gained any great significance for Welles's parents, or the moment any weight. Maybe it can be no other way with our understanding. It was a common instant of the sort we experience and simultaneously forget, until we somehow retrieve it and assign it value. So many moments would be retrieved this way, recovered from the sea bottom of time past. What emerges, brought back to the surface and lifted to the light, will always be a bit suspect, subject to the dangers attached to all we recollect: to invention and exaggeration, to mythmaking and foreshadowing. Little of it rises to the point of pure, indisputable truth. It seems the smaller the moment, the closer we get.

One gesture abides in Alison and Jeff's memory from that evening, a simple act, reflexive and even a little vain. Walking in front of his parents on the sidewalk, Welles reached into his back pocket for a comb to fix his hair. They weren't surprised. He carried a comb for most of his life.

"Welles, are you *still* carrying that thing?" Alison asked.

She wasn't talking about the comb. She was talking about the red bandanna wrapped around it. She couldn't remember the last time she'd actually seen him with it.

She laughed. "Here you are," she said. "Living in the city. Working on Wall Street. And you're still carrying around a red bandanna?" *Just like his father, to this day* was the next thought in her head. Sure enough, Jeff was carrying a blue bandanna in his back pocket, the way he always did. Red for Welles, blue for Jeff.

"Of course, I still carry it," Welles said, smiling. "Absolutely."

And then, after combing his hair, he placed it back into the centerfold of the handkerchief, and put the bandanna back into his pocket.

To carry and keep, as he had for the last seventeen years.

The picture of the boy was taken at Alison's parents' house. The boy is maybe eight years old. He beams up from the linoleum floor of the kitchen in his blue jeans and daffodil shirt, his digital watch on his wrist and brown boots on his feet. Behind him, a wooden chair shows him its back, next to a pair of disembodied legs flaring up to some unseen torso.

He is beautiful, as is all he signifies: guilelessness and joy, the world open to him. His legs are bent; he squats in position, his hands on his knees, his chest leaning forward and his chin uplifted. The next moment is an adventure so great in possibility that he bends at the waist to meet it.

From before this age, the father has called him by a nickname: "old man." Old man, he says, from the time the two can hold conversations. Old man, want to go to McDonald's for some lunch? Old man, want to come with me to the firehouse? Old man, what do you think?

The boy laughs. He loves The Incredible Hulk and The Dukes of Hazzard, figures with capes and conquerors with superpowers. He loves action without needing to call it by a name. It's every day's awakening.

And in the picture displayed in his mind and pinned to the album, the father sees the smile and the virtue and the radiance. And he sees what we all see when we look with him. There already in the photo is the bright sash across the boy's forehead. The red bandanna's fold is generous and thick, trapping his blondish bangs underneath its top edge. The knot tied behind his head, its tail sticks from behind his ear, looming over his shoulder in a dash, a flat line.

For the father, the picture calls forth a simple one-word caption. In the boy's posture, in his open face and eight-year-old frame, in his smile and his lean forward, it's already there, in the cells of his being—the attitude and the code, the call and the reply.

Two syllables. One word.

Ready.

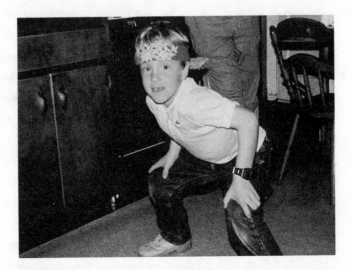

II

WHAT WOULD YOU DO IN THE LAST HOUR OF YOUR LIFE?

Where would you be?

What would it look like?

Who would remember it?

If you could know, would you want to? Would you receive that knowledge with dread, or accept it with grace? Would there be a peace to be gained, or one already granted?

If you understood the mortal clock, what would you trade to gain another hour, and then another after that? What prayer would you recite, what deal would you make, what promise would you offer, for this not to be the end?

Look upon the common fears of what your final hour might be. Take the typical conditions and likely circumstances. You know them, you've seen them, you've lost others to them. The ebbing mind or failing body. The loss of family and lack of purpose. The fact of pain or the regimen of medicines. In a home not your own, in the prisons of old age, receiving the full force of its sentencing, there might be a mercy in the dulling of your intellect. After seven or eight or nine decades, maybe the final hour feels like reward.

But imagine it's sooner. It's an instant from now, one blink from current, it's the line after the line you're reading. The decades haven't stacked like wood for the winter, and the years haven't collected in enough albums. You haven't reached any golden age, or twilight time. You're not winding down or scaling back, not going gray or getting slow. You're not there yet. You're not close. You're not old.

For you, legacy is a distant and irrelevant word; it's for obituaries and sports columns. You're twenty-four. You're ready. You're young. The hours are yours, until the last one arrives.

If you knew this might be that time, this could be the end, this may be the very last hour you have to spend, what would you do?

And what if the hour, with all its horror and loss, its panic and shock, still somehow gave you a choice—to fly from risk, to escape, to live?

What would you do, then, in the last hour of your life?

B lue.
So deep it was an occasion.

The vault of sky that morning was boundless and crystal, a shade so brilliant it would set the day, and after, pierce its memory.

The night before, a cold front pushed down from Canada and swept across parts of the East Coast, carrying rain and thunderstorms with it. Fresh cool air came behind, bringing unclouded skies the next dawn.

After the humidity and swelter of August, the morning was unseasonably cool, a gift to everyone stepping outside. Winds were gentle, and temperatures were in the low 60s at seven A.M. in the city, and predicted to climb no higher than 75 at the peak of the day.

The visibility was limitless.

From sunrise, September 11, 2001, was a perfect day for flying.

A lison was no stranger to premonitions.

They started when she was sixteen years old, still in high school. As alien and sudden visions they came, without any interpreter or code. She was uncertain how to react to them at first, beyond the cold knife of fear. Were they meant to be understood as warnings or instruction, as signs to guide toward or away from the next given hour or day? How would others judge her for receiving the visions? Could she describe or explain them without sounding absurd? Should she let anyone know? How would she respond if they doubted or dismissed them? Or her? She learned to accept them, trying to interpret their meaning rather than deny their power.

But the night of September 10 was something else. The anxiety came on with a force she'd never experienced. It was pushing her past worry, into panic.

She thought she was falling apart. Getting out of bed, going downstairs, she tried to calm herself by writing her feelings down on the computer, but the screen appeared fragmented to her. She went back upstairs, into bed, and tried to sleep. It was fruitless.

Up before six, she decided to go for an early morning workout at a fitness club. She would be spending the day at her office in Briarcliff Manor, New York, planning for an upcoming business meeting with the president of the company she worked for. She left before the peak of the rush hour arrived. Driving across the Tappan Zee Bridge, the premonition came to her again, this time in a sentence.

You're going to die today, the voice said to her.

"I felt like my chest opened up," she recounted years later, "and a brilliant light shot out. I'm suddenly in this cloudy place above myself, but I was in complete serene and utter peace." It was 7:00 A.M. on the morning of September 11. Alison continued to drive across the bridge beneath the blue dome of sky.

Jeff Crowther was going golfing. The bank where he worked had purchased the tee time in a benefit outing scheduled to begin later in the morning. It was the usual agenda. Breakfast. Pairings. Driving range. Shotgun start. Drinks and prizes after the round. A good day for a man who didn't get enough days on the links. Jeff was making his final preparations, getting ready to leave the house, when the phone rang. It was his older brother Bosley, calling from Virginia.

"Hey, are you watching TV?"

Jimmy Dunne was already playing golf early that morning, to the surprise of exactly no one who knew him. The game registered somewhere between fixation and mania for Dunne, and he practiced and played that way. As a pursuit, this fit his general worldview and life's philosophy. Do everything, all the time, absolutely as hard as you can. Golf can prove resistant to such an approach. For most, a talent for the game needs a measure of conjuring, or nurturing. Dunne didn't traffic in such beliefs. Forty-four years old, he believed the world largely yielded to will. Much of his life, and his game, was proof.

Growing up in Babylon on Long Island, he played his early rounds on the municipal courses nearby, like Dix Hills and Sunken

Meadow, and caddied before he became a teenager, before his family joined Southward Ho Country Club in Bay Shore.

As he climbed his way through a career, with success coming quickly as a Wall Street bond trader, his passion for the game deepened. With that success came access to some of the greatest courses in the world, the ones that inspired envy and awe for the legions who would never play them. In time, he would be a member at Pine Valley, Shinnecock Hills, and Augusta National.

Dunne's obsession with golf likely saved his life. The night before, he told his mentor, Herman Sandler, that he wasn't coming into the office the next morning. Sandler hardly needed to ask where Dunne would be. He worked hard enough at golf to possess a 1-handicap, trending toward scratch, and was trying to qualify for the United States Mid-Amateur Championship for the first time.

Created for nonprofessionals over the age of twenty-five, the event was designed to be a venue for players who had careers and families, not PGA Tour cards and endorsement contracts. It gave strong players with otherwise busy lives a prize to chase. Run by the United States Golf Association, it drew elite amateurs into competition against one another. The championship was set for a club course in Fresno, California, the second week of October, barely a month away. Dunne was determined to qualify.

That morning, he was at the Bedford Golf and Tennis Club, an hour north of New York City, already on his sixth or seventh hole of the day. A man with a walkie-talkie approached him. The intrusion during a round was unusual for any golfer, and borderline heresy for Dunne. Immediately, it drew his mind to worry if something had happened to his family.

"Are my kids okay? Is my wife okay?"

Yes.

Assuming the matter was not urgent, Dunne turned back to the hole and played two more shots, until the man with the walkie-talkie grew insistent. "You need to call your office," he said. "Now.

"This has nothing to do with business. A plane hit your building."

They came to the towers that morning with their birthmarks and degrees, allegiances and scars, student loans and night cravings. They came with their loves cherished and lost, fights joined and surrendered, bills paid and put off. They came from different paths, took different chances, practiced different faiths, savored different meals. They came with deals made, lines drawn, ventures failed, disciplines mastered, addictions enabled, orders given, cheers shouted, ideas grasped, fears hidden, reports filed, hours wasted, hearts thrilled, children birthed, time served, hopes lost. Breaths taken. Breaths held.

There were 14,154 people in the World Trade Center that morning. It was a city unto itself. The towers totaled 220 floors of Manhattan real estate. Each floor was nearly an acre of space— roughly equivalent to the size of a football field, the fields were stacked on top of each other, separated by twelve feet of steel and a floor number.

They arrived from every direction, after grueling commutes on the Long Island Expressway and traffic clogs in the Holland Tunnel, by the lettered and numbered lines of the subway, in the PATH trains sliding beneath the Hudson and on the Staten Island Ferry churning across its waters, out of the gridlocked streets east of the Battery and out of cabs that stopped along West Street.

Welles was one among the fourteen thousand. He left his apartment on Washington Place in the West Village around seven that morning, as he usually did, his suit and tie straight out of the cleaner's plastic. From the time he started at Sandler, he liked to arrive at the office early to get a jump on the day, for the impression it created, and for the savings. The firm often served a great breakfast spread, and Welles didn't like to miss out. The food was good, and the price was better.

It was little more than a mile and a half from his door to the entrances of 2 World Trade, his tower. There were different ways to make the commute, depending on the day, the weather, the mood, the first meeting. He could hoof it over to the subway station at Christopher Street and Sheridan Square along Seventh Avenue, less than a five-minute walk from the apartment. There he'd disappear from the street, down the steps, to catch the southbound local, the 1 train. He could step out of his building and hop in a cab if he wanted to save a bit of time and spend a bit more pocket cash, but he'd need some luck to find an empty taxi in the morning rush.

Or, on a morning like this, he might have walked. Either way, he didn't want to be late.

He was gone.

When Chuck Platz woke up on the morning of September 11, Welles had already left the apartment. Platz's bedroom was next to the bathroom, and often he heard the sounds of his roommate's morning rituals, the shower and shave that started his day. In this regard, Welles was considerate of his cotenant, down to the detail of often waiting to put his shoes on only after leaving the apartment, to minimize the noise.

The first signal came more than an hour after Welles had closed the door, when Platz was in the bathroom. He'd long ago grown used to the din of the city; it was an unconscious static, a frequency he'd learned to block but for the shrillest notes. He was standing at the bathroom sink, shaving, when he heard a sound that shook the bones of the room itself, rattling the glass in the mirror, a roar that forced him to tense his upper body, as if bracing for a blow. It was an airplane.

As if following the sound, Platz left the bathroom, walked into the bedroom, and looked south from the window. As he had done so many times before, he found the spot that granted the best vantage of the Trade Center. He saw the tops of the towers. One of them was on fire.

He rushed to get dressed and headed down the five flights out the entryway of the building and onto the street. The first person who spoke to him was a crossing guard for the Academy of St. Joseph, an elementary school next to the apartment building. He could hear others already talking about a bomb going off downtown, or accounts of a small plane hitting one of the towers, but the guard, still looking skyward, was definitive.

"That wasn't a bomb," she said. "It was a big plane."

For an instant, or perhaps it was a minute—it was an interval he'd never be able to measure or forget—he stood still on Washington Place, lost, staring at the burning hole on the face of the North Tower, like so many others around him. The sight was at once vivid and impossible, a vision beyond comprehension, yet demanding of some urgent response.

His mind cleared with a single name: Welles.

. . .

Natalie McIver was tired. The pregnancy was thrilling, of course, but also exhausting, and by the last trimester there were mornings when it was difficult to summon the energy to start the day and all its routines, to get up, get herself together, get dressed, get out the door, and get down to the ferry to make the trip across the river, to get into the lobby and get the elevator and go all the way up to very near the top of the South Tower.

She had another reason to be tired. For the past two and a half weeks, she'd been working without one of her key colleagues by her side. Sharon Moore, a vice president and research analyst at Sandler, had taken a vacation in advance of McIver's maternity leave. She would be out for an extended time—her plan was to take three months—and Moore wanted to get her own R&R in before she left.

The two understood each other's schedules and worked well together. Typically, they worked a type of split shift. One always had to be in especially early, by seven, to cover premarket open meetings, and would then leave the office by four, at least in theory. The other would come in later, by nine, and head out by five-thirty or six. They traded back and forth between the shifts.

The past two weeks without Moore were hard for McIver. She was past seven months pregnant, coming in early and staying late, essentially covering both shifts. She knew it was part of the deal, but still, it was tiring. She had been working on the details of a conference scheduled for September 13 at Le Parker Meridien hotel in Midtown, arranging the logistics for all those planning to attend—guests, bankers, speakers, and the firm's senior leadership. Her plan was to come in at seven the entire week. She didn't want to burden Moore, just coming back from vacation, by dumping a truckload of details on her desk about a conference happening in two days.

But today, finally, was Moore's first day back from vacation, and despite McIver's intention to be in early, her body argued for another hour of sleep. She listened to it, deciding she would make it in by nine. After getting up and out of the apartment in Jersey City, almost directly across the Hudson from the Trade Center, she made the walk to the ferry for the ride across the river. She'd be glad to see Moore, to hear about her vacation and catch up a bit about her teenage son, Lance, and of course to get some needed reinforcement for the work ahead.

She stepped on the ferry for the short trip east, taking in the magnificence of the day. On the water, she heard a strange thunder in the blue sky.

She looked up, and saw the plane. It was very low.

Ling Young was walking across very familiar ground. She was an auditor for the New York State Department of Taxation and Finance, an agency that had called the Trade Center home almost since the towers' inception, with a hiatus during the nineties when it relocated to Brooklyn. The department returned to Lower Manhattan in 1999, claiming space on the 86th and 87th floors of the South Tower.

Young's work was primarily out in the field, performing audits on individuals and corporations, handling all manner of tax-return compliance issues. Today, she was coming in, and heading up to the 86th floor.

Forty-nine years old, she still found her trips to the Trade Center vaguely exciting, the complex buzzing with humanity, so many lives crossing in its concourses and open spaces. Her only apprehension, if there was any, was rooted in the 1993 terrorist attack there, when the offices were across the East River. She was grateful not to have been in the towers that February day, but the terror of it all still registered with her, if dimly, when she reported to 2 World Trade.

Young reached her office before eight A.M. Less than an hour later, she was talking with a supervisor when their conversation broke off in midsentence. Each looked at the other, startled into silence. She swore the sound was an explosion.

Judy Wein was in earlier than Ling Young and stationed higher in the building. Wein, forty-five years old, a senior vice president at Aon Corporation, had been with the company in its different identities since 1978, earning an MBA as she rose to the executive suite. That September morning, she commuted in from Queens with her husband, Gerry Sussman, as they did most workdays. Gerry was an appeals officer for the Internal Revenue Service, and Judy was in risk assessment for Aon, doing actuarial work. For Judy, the work was both rewarding and grinding; she was a significant producer, typically billing eighteen hundred hours or more a year. That volume required long days, usually starting before seven A.M. and not wrapping until after six P.M.

That morning, after getting to Lower Manhattan, the couple walked together to City Hall and stopped to kiss each other goodbye. Judy went off to her corner office on the 103rd floor of 2

World Trade. Her view faced west, out over the Hudson to New Jersey, and on a day this clear, seemingly beyond. Toward the north, a part of 1 World Trade blocked a stretch of horizon. She ate breakfast in the office, a healthy plate of yogurt and fruit. The early stages of the day held nothing more than the ordinary rituals and requirements of her high-powered job, and soon she found herself under the spell of the numbers that governed her working life. It could take an unusual sound to break the trance. About an hour and a half after she arrived that morning, she heard such a noise—a massive boom coming right outside the window.

She looked up instantly in its direction.

That's when she saw the enormous ball of fire rising from below.

John Ryan was to meet an informant that morning. The spot they set was downtown, in a vast, bustling place, strategically anonymous and far away from the subjects they would discuss. They'd convene somewhere in the World Trade Center complex.

It was a place Ryan knew well, long before he'd joined the Port Authority Police Department. Growing up in the Red Hook neighborhood of Brooklyn, he had pursued a passion with a deep history in the borough, a hobby he kept despite all the other, more modern distractions calling to a teenager in the city. Ryan liked to keep and fly pigeons.

The rooftops of south Brooklyn were a working center of the pigeon-flying subculture, filled with makeshift coops, wood-and-wire shacks, and lean-tos. For some of the men who kept pigeons, the pursuit had all the demands of a part-time job, from the hours they spent feeding and watering the birds to keeping them and their quarters at least partially clean to training the pigeons to fly their routes and find their way back.

It led to moments of great serenity, times when the birds lit out from their coops, winging over the confining streets and into the freedom of air and sky. They soared, and the birdmen of Brooklyn followed the patterns of their flights.

When Ryan looked out across the rooftops, eyes trained west, the towers were always there to fix the horizon, familiar yet magnetic, drawing his gaze. Maybe that's why, at seventeen, he crossed the river to work there. Not merely inside the buildings, but as close to the top as he could. Ryan got a job as a guide, working the observation deck at 2 World Trade Center.

The North Tower, 1 World Trade, had its restaurant, Windows on the World, a breathtaking venue on the 106th and 107th floors, serving three meals a day at high prices with incomparable views. The South Tower's answer was its Top of the World observatories, two observation decks, on its 107th and 110th floors. The space on 107 was indoors, with wider windows and smaller columns, to allow for the best viewing experience. For those who wanted to climb higher still, depending on the weather, escalators carried visitors up another three stories to the 110th floor and a greater thrill—stepping outside onto a platform to behold the vistas in open air. The deck was 1,377 feet above street level. There weren't many pigeons interrupting the panorama.

A friend from the neighborhood suggested Ryan apply for the part-time gig. The job proved perfect, and also placed him in the spot where he'd build his career. WTC served as the headquarters for the Port Authority of New York and New Jersey, a joint venture between the states overseeing all the transportation infrastructure of the region—from its seaports and airports to many of its tunnels and bridges. A vast governmental agency, it included its own police force with more than fifteen hundred officers. As he entered college, Ryan's interest moved toward law enforcement. The authority's headquarters were located in the North Tower.

After attending college, and then graduating from the police academy, Ryan started with the Port Authority Police Department in 1979. His first assignment was at JFK International Airport in Queens. Eventually, he was transferred to Manhattan and the Port Authority Bus Terminal on Eighth Avenue near Forty-second street. Times Square. He spent more than twenty years on the assignment.

For most of those years, the terminal was in the center of a strip of X-rated movie theaters and peep shows, a neon-lit underbelly attracting every flavor of hoodlum and every brand of crime. The western edge of the neighborhood was its worst, with Eighth Avenue the darkest vein, pulsing with the rough trades of prostitution and drug dealing, and the attendant shootings and stabbings. The sprawling bus station was the stage set for all sorts of greater or lesser crimes.

There was also an entrenched and expanding gang problem moving through the Hell's Kitchen neighborhood and infecting the terminal. Ryan was working on that issue with the help of his informant. To protect the informant's confidentiality, they had arranged to meet downtown, away from Times Square.

In making the appointment, however, Ryan had forgotten about the family calendar. The eleventh was the first day of his daughter's preschool out on Long Island. He needed to be home in time to take his daughter to the school's afternoon session. The meeting at the World Trade Center was rescheduled.

Ryan asked for the day off. But that morning, the phone rang, and he went straight to work.

He would not have another day off for the next eight months.

Eighty-three people were in the offices at Sandler O'Neill that morning—men and women, mothers and fathers, war veterans and MBAs, founding principals and executive assistants, underperformers and rainmakers, Little League coaches and marathon runners, surrounded by the blue sky, beginning to sort through the demands of the day. For most, it was a time to settle in—readying for the meetings and reports, the trades and positions, the e-mails and calls that would shape the nine or ten hours ahead across a cloudless Tuesday.

8:46:40 A.M.
Impact.

American Airlines Flight 11 out of Boston, a Boeing 767 jet with eighty-one passengers and eleven crew aboard, was carrying 10,000 gallons of fuel and traveling at 465 miles per hour when it crashed into the North Tower of the World Trade Center.

The jet slammed into the north side of the building, killing all ninety-two on board as it exploded through seven floors of the tower. It measured 156 feet across its wingspan, the jet's left tip blasting through the 93rd floor, while its right ripped through the 99th. The path of destruction ran directly through the offices of a single corporation, the Marsh & McLennan Companies, an insurance and professional services firm. Hundreds were killed instantly by the impact, without ever having known what ended their lives.

The force of the crash was so great, parts of the plane's landing gear burst out the south side of the tower, opposite where the plane entered, flying the length of five city blocks through the air before landing in the street. The plane's fuel ignited on impact with the building, triggering an explosive fire, scorching all it touched in its spread as it roared from the open wounds of the building, sending out a blast of heat strong enough to singe the blue itself.

Chuck Platz reached for his phone and dialed. The call went straight to voice mail. He tried again. Same.

His next impulse was simple: Go. Go there. Get to him. Get on the subway and head south to Chambers Street, up and out to the plaza, to find a way to reach Welles. Or walk or run there, through the chaos. The moment held as much uncertainty as urgency, maybe more. He didn't stop to calculate whether the smoke he saw in the moment was pouring from the tower closer to him or farther away, whether it was World Trade Center 1 or 2, the North Tower or the South.

He headed toward the subway, but then heard the announcement. Downtown service was already being suspended. He turned around and headed back to 115 Washington.

If he heard the second plane hit, or understood that its target was the South Tower, Platz can only recall walking into the building and making his way upward, past the apartment on the fifth floor, until he reached the roof. The smoke from the towers was flooding outward now and blurring the city's skyline before his eyes. He continued to call Welles, without success. At one point, he left a message, forcing himself to sound casual and matter-of-fact. "Hey, make sure you're okay. I'll meet you at Boxers tonight."

Standing on the rooftop of the building, he wondered what he could do. He remembered he had a disposable camera in his bag, and, lacking any other way to help, he raised the plastic shell, looked through its hollow view, and snapped a picture looking south. It would be years before he found the courage to develop the film.

A short time later, standing in the same spot, he saw the first tower fall. He didn't know whether it was the North or the South Tower, the one where Welles worked or the one he looked at from his 104th floor office. He didn't know if Welles was inside or outside, trapped or free, headed home by then, or never again.

Platz was paralyzed by what he saw and couldn't understand, what he feared and didn't know. "People asked me if, in my heart of hearts, I knew," Platz said. "My mind wouldn't allow itself to form a thought."

Something primal kept his rising panic at bay: hope.

. . .

Only 131 feet separated the towers—less than half a football field of open space between a furnace of flame erupting from the gashes of one structure and the gleaming façade of the other.

Inside the South Tower, people on the highest floors facing west could feel the extreme heat through their office windows, its swelter touching their cheeks and the sleeves of their shirts. In the first several minutes after Flight 11 hit the North Tower, confusion ruled everywhere, including in the South Tower, where even those facing away from the plane's entry point felt the reverberations of the crash. Many who could see the damage assumed that a small plane or helicopter had flown into the building. The smoke made it hard to absorb the scope of the devastation.

In her office at Sandler O'Neill, on the 104th floor of the South Tower, Karen Fishman was talking with Gordon Aamoth, who had just made key progress on an enormous and complicated merger he'd been working on for years. It was the biggest deal of his career at the firm, set to be announced that week. That's when she heard Herman Sandler, and perhaps Chris Quackenbush as well, two of the firm's three leaders, make the announcement that a plane had hit the North Tower.

She ran out of her office into Quackenbush's to see what happened. A truly panoramic view wasn't possible in the towers, particularly up close. Its windows were less than two feet wide, just eighteen inches across. The towers' architect, Minoru Yamasaki, suffered from a fear of heights. The narrow office windows, with pillars on either side, restricted the views. Fishman's view from the windows in Quackenbush's office was complicated by a storm of paper blowing through the air and a growing cloud of smoke.

Mark Fitzgibbon had been Welles's boss on the research side of Sandler until Welles moved to the trading desk. He was in his office that morning, meeting with his colleague John Kline, both of them oblivious to anything happening outside, when the two heard a commotion outside the door. The office was next to a stairwell leading out of Sandler's offices. Opening the door, he smelled what he believed were the first few wisps of smoke. He saw a few people quickly moving toward the stairs, and assumed it was a fire.

At the same time, Stephen Joseph, one of the firm's managing directors, heard an unusual sound from his spot at the trading desk, but quickly dismissed it. The firm's trading floor faced away from the North Tower, and he'd learned long before to block out distractions during the workday to concentrate on the cascade of decisions and calculations that governed market hours. But when he heard an announcement from Ken McBrayer, principal in charge of mortgage finance and a Naval Academy graduate, Joseph heard the angst in his voice. He got up immediately and headed for the windows. Even before getting there, he knew: I'm not staying. Walking back to his desk, he turned to Andy Cott and Jace Day, two of his colleagues on the desk, and was blunt.

"You've got little kids," Joseph said. "I have little kids. We should leave. Now."

For many of the firm's veteran employees, like Karen Fishman, the announcement triggered memories of the terrorist attack in 1993, and the conflicting sets of directions they'd received in its immediate aftermath. Even though it was more than eight years before, the anxiety of the day never completely faded.

"I was there," Fishman recalled, "and even though you were better off doing nothing, I knew you couldn't trust the building. You

couldn't trust its management. The whole place was just a mess."
Eight years earlier, she and thousands of others in both towers
received contradictory orders on when to evacuate, or whether to
leave at all. For those on the highest floors, like Sandler, the result
was a long and confusing day, waiting to learn what to do. It ended
with a harrowing walk down the building's stairwells in the pitch
dark, many holding on to the shoulders of those directly in front
of them to follow their lead.

Herman Sandler tried to be clear and calm in the instructions
he gave to all in the office this morning. They had not been given
any official evacuation order yet. No one *had* to leave. But anyone
who felt uncomfortable at all and wanted to leave should absolutely go.

And so the boundary line was drawn, though no one could
see it.

To stay or leave, to follow an instinct or adhere to a schedule—
this, now, was the hinge point between living and dying.

For the eighty-three people in the office, what voice inside spoke
to them, and what did it say? Some dropped everything and exited.
Others called or heard from loved ones while at their desks. Who
was guided by the immediate reactions of those next to them, and
who made the choice independently and quickly?

No one could know, not in the ways knowledge presents itself
to us—in facts and proofs, with data or experience—none possessed the truth that every additional second spent on the floor
was a move closer to death. On the 104th floor, some heard a
voice or had a sense or made a choice before or after hearing Herman Sandler issue his instructions. Already, they were making

their way toward the elevators or into the stairwell near Fitzgibbon's office.

They were taking the first steps to their survival.

Before nine A.M., Welles was at his desk when the phone rang. It was his friend and former roommate Johnny Howells. Howells was in Boston, at work in his home office. Minutes earlier he'd been on a conference call when his housemate interrupted to tell him a plane had hit the World Trade Center. Howells muted the line, looked to the television, and saw smoke pouring from one of the buildings. *Oh my God.*

He got back on the line, telling others on the call he had a friend working in the towers. He had to go. Despite the visit he made with Welles to the offices at Sandler on that quiet Sunday afternoon a year before, when Welles was so proud to show off the views from the 104th floor, Howells couldn't remember which tower they visited. Where was the office? Was it the North Tower or the South? Where was Welles right now?

He picked up the phone and, still watching the dark clouds surging out of the building on his television screen, dialed Welles's desk number. Almost immediately, the line picked up. Welles answered. Howells was stunned.

"Welles," he said, "are you all right?"

"Yeah, I'm fine," Welles replied. His voice was clear. "It was the other building."

"Get out of there," Howells said, without hesitating.

"I think we're okay," Welles answered. If there was any edge in his voice, Howells didn't hear it. "Something hit the other building. You could feel it, but I'm all right."

Howells, along with millions of others across the country and around the world, were seeing the first images of the devastation to the North Tower, the first seeds of catastrophe unfolding in real time in their living rooms and kitchens and offices. One hundred two minutes after being struck, the building would collapse to the ground.

But when Howells called Welles was 131 feet away from the burning North Tower, and had only a vague sense of its condition or the chaos spreading through its upper floors. He couldn't see people breaking out the tower's windows, some perched there, others leaping to their deaths.

Howells repeated himself, more forcefully this time.

"Get out of there."

"Actually, they're coming on now," Welles said, referring to an announcement being made over the office speakers. "They're saying we are going to get out of here so . . . I'll give you a call later." The call ended there.

The evacuation order came across the public address system in the office.

It was 9:02 A.M.

Through the South Tower's PA speakers, the Port Authority broadcast the message:

"May I have your attention, please. Repeating this message: the situation occurred in Building 1. If the conditions warrant on your floor, you may wish to start an orderly evacuation."

One minute later.

   9:03:02 A.M.

United Airlines Flight 175, another Boeing 767 jet out of Boston, flying northward at a speed estimated between 540 and 590 miles per hour, losing altitude at a rate of 5,000 feet per minute during its final nosedive, banked at the last second before slamming into the South Tower. Upon striking the south side of the building, all sixty-five on board were killed instantly. The oldest passenger was eighty years old; the youngest, not yet three.

The plane, carrying a nearly full load of 10,000 gallons of fuel, tilted its left wing down just as it hurled itself into the building. The wings sliced through seven floors of the tower at the initial crash point, the impact zone running from the 78th to the 84th floors. Upon hitting the façade, its jet fuel ignited, spreading across space, bursting into savage fires and sending out waves of broiling heat.

The entire tower rocked with the force of the crash, shaking from its top floor down to its foundation and below, pulsing into the bedrock. The building pitched hard in one direction before its steel core bent back the other way, swaying violently from side to side. Eventually the vibrations subsided and the tower remained standing, regaining its central balance.

The plane's nose crashed into the 81st floor at the first point of impact, a place in the tower holding a concentration of heavy elevator machinery. The fuselage rapidly disintegrated as it plowed into the machinery's immense bulk. Through most of the building, the three main stairwells were bunched close to one another, and close to the building's center. Here, in the impact zone, the stairwells were spread out, closer to the edges of the tower, to make room for the hulking elevator machinery, which took up so much space on these floors.

As a result, Stairway A, the stairwell in the northwest corner of the tower, farthest from where the plane entered the building, withstood the devastating effects of the crash. It remained intact.

These stairs were the sole path down. For most in the impact zone and above, those who survived the obliterating violence of the crash, the stairs could reset the boundary.

They were the way out—if anyone could find them.

Mark Fitzgibbon, John Kline, and Karen Fishman were already well on their way down that stairwell. After the first plane hit the North Tower, each made the decision to leave quickly. Fitzgibbon hesitated for a moment, but saw Fishman in the hallway, and she urged him to go. She also told him not to take the elevator. She remembered people being stuck inside the cars for hours, having to be discovered and freed during the 1993 attack. In the blast, a truck bomb detonated in a garage beneath the complex, killing six and injuring more than a thousand.

If Stephen Joseph, Jace Day, and Andy Cott shared Fishman's misgivings about the elevators, they ignored them. Joseph, a Harvard graduate and Vietnam veteran, heard the echo of his military training: in a crisis, get to a position of safety first. Only there can you best evaluate the threat and be in position to react and respond. Less than ten minutes after Flight 11 struck the North Tower, Joseph and his colleagues stepped into an elevator outside Sandler's offices and went directly down to the sky lobby on the 78th floor.

Stepping off, they looked to transfer to a different bank of cars heading the rest of the way down to the ground floor. The first car was full. They moved to another car, which quickly filled up as they stepped inside, and went directly down to the tower's lobby.

More than sixty floors above, Fishman and Fitzgibbon were continuing to make their descent through Stairway A. The stairwell was growing more crowded, but the atmosphere wasn't edgy or panicked. Fishman also saw a smaller group of civilians, office workers who were climbing back up. They had reversed course from their descent. Likely, some had heard the Port Authority's announcement at 8:55 A.M. instructing tenants to remain in the building:

"Your attention, please, ladies and gentlemen. Building 2 is secure. There is no need to evacuate Building 2. If you are in the midst of evacuation, you may use the reentry doors and the elevators to return to your office. Repeat. Building 2 is secure."

On the 68th floor, Fishman saw a fire marshal echoing the message, telling people in the stairwell it was safe to go back upstairs. The incident was confined to the other tower. She paused for a moment, then disregarded the instruction, walking past him and continuing downward.

Just a few floors farther down on her trip, a few moments later, Flight 175 slammed into the South Tower. Sixteen minutes had passed since the first plane struck the North Tower. Mark Fitzgibbon, also in the stairwell, was immediately thrown from his feet, his body crashing into a wall, as the building shook from side to side. He could sense the entire structure around him rocking back and forth, and briefly wondered if the tower could stand. Eventually, he found his way back to his feet and, along with the others around him, regained his bearings and began moving down the flights as fast as he could, with urgency now, taking the steps three and four at a time.

John Kline was also moving as quickly as he could, now sensing with a terrible clarity that the buildings were under attack. Even as he gained ground, moving closer to the ground-floor lobby with each step, the stairwells were growing more crowded, the pace

slowing, the line backing up, and people pressing into one another. His prime thought was that he wouldn't make it. He would
never get out, never reach home. He would die in the tower. He
thought of his wife and his children, of what they would do without him.

Soon, he, Joseph, and Fishman would reach the lobby, and despite the debris raining down from the skies outside and those
who were leaping to their deaths from the fires of the North
Tower, they would push forward to safety. They didn't know it,
but they were no longer just part of Sandler's eighty-three, the
number of people who were in the office that day; they'd joined a
very different group, the seventeen who survived.

After dialing his father's office line there was no obvious note
of panic in his voice as he left a message with a secretary to
assure him he was all right. Jeff would certainly check in upon
hearing about the plane crash, and he'd have the message waiting.

Next, he called his mother on her cell phone. For some reason,
Alison never heard the call. It went straight to voice mail. Welles
left a short message.

"Mom . . . this is Welles. I . . . I want you to know that I'm
okay."

The time was 9:12 A.M. They were the last words his family
would ever hear him speak.

There, a curtain falls. Behind it dwell uncertainty and mystery. Beyond the last calls taken, the last messages left, the
last words heard, there is a gulley, where hope and belief mix in

the shadows. There, it's guesswork. The unknown pushes and taunts, driving investigation, but only so far, until it reaches the curtain. Past it, there is ether and theory, not the truth of fact. So much lies past knowing.

When Flight 175 tore its way through the floors beneath him, when the tower reeled back and forth, testing the limits of its steel skeleton and the principles of its design, what went through his mind then? The instant the jet made impact with the south face of the building, did he allow himself to think that it was too late? Was he already looking backward, regretting his decision not to leave when the others left?

Why didn't he go? Perhaps those around him, the ones who endured the 1993 attack, advised against it. Many felt the best course then had been to stay put, to continue working. It was those who left sooner who endured a harder, longer slog down the stairs. There were also those who went up to the roof only to freeze in the February air, and then be forced to make their way back down the stairs anyway.

Why didn't he go? It could've been the undefeated faith of the young, the wrap of impregnability that comes from being vital, strong, ascendant. He knew about danger, not from some action movie or drama series. He'd lived it with Empire, answering the calls and donning the gear. He wasn't made or trained to run away from peril but to go toward it.

Why didn't he go? There is the simplest reason. Because he didn't know, because there was no way to understand, that moments away, a 767 jet was bearing down on the piece of sky where he and thousands of others stood at the beginning of their day.

Why didn't he go? Later, he did. He left the office on the 104th floor, heading down. The path appeared clear. He was in Stairway A.

．　．　．

Soon after hearing the boom from the first plane striking the North Tower, Ling Young felt heat penetrating the department offices on the 86th floor of the South Tower. She didn't know what happened, but feeling the heat was trigger enough. She and others around her made the decision to leave.

The small group got in an elevator on 86, heading down to the sky lobby on the 78th floor, for the transfer to the express elevators to the lobby. The elevators were enormous, the size of a room, with enough space to fit fifty-five people. The cars were designed to cover the 78 floors down to street level, 844 vertical feet, in less than a minute. Crowded with people just arriving for the day's work, there were perhaps a hundred or more in the area ready to switch to local elevators for the upper floors, and others, like Young, looking to go back down.

There were no cars open for the trip down. Young's group waited among the larger crowd, and began to talk. Like everyone in the lobby, they were stalled there, suspended between going up and coming down. Some of her colleagues were trying to figure out the cause of the explosion in the North Tower. No one knew for sure. One suggested going back up to 86, to see if they might call the governor's office for more information. They also heard the announcement over the building's PA system telling people to return to their offices, as the incident was confined to the other tower. Young was firm. The burning smell was growing a bit stronger, faintly like burned rubber, or at least that was the sense she had. She was going down.

A car appeared, its doors opening. As she and the others stepped toward it, the wing of Flight 175 burst through the wall. The lobby exploded.

Whatever the dimensions of hell, Young landed inside them. The impact had thrown her from one end of the elevator lobby to the other. Uncertain if she'd ever lost consciousness, she lay on the floor nearly smothered in dust and debris for what felt like minutes before trying to lift herself up. Fires burned a small distance away, in the middle of the lobby, and flames were shooting out from the elevator shafts. There was black smoke choking the air, and piles of what looked like shattered plaster scattered everywhere. The walls and ceiling of the lobby vaporized, huge banks of windows shattered, the entire space disintegrating at the moment the plane entered, its force an obliteration. She wondered if she'd been blinded, only to realize her glasses were covered in blood, like much of the rest of her. She reached down to her shirt, using the fabric to wipe them off. When she put her glasses back on, the sight overwhelmed her.

She was surrounded by scores of the dead and dying. Next to her was a man whose facial features had been shorn off his skull. A few feet away, she saw a woman whose legs had been severed. Bodies filled the remnants of the floor, stacked atop and beneath the shattered walls. There were limbs and torsos torn apart by the jet's impact, others charred beyond recognition by the explosion of the jet fuel. Moments earlier, she had been waiting to board the open elevator, hearing conversations course and echo through the lobby. Now so many of those lives were silenced, motionless. The massacre was beyond understanding. Nearly everywhere she looked was death. She gazed down at her body. Her own injuries and severe burns didn't register; there was no pain, the hurt smothered by shock.

She continued to sit where she was, on a portion of the floor still intact, uncertain what to do. If she moved, she worried the entire floor would collapse beneath her. She heard sounds, signs of life, and understood she wasn't alone. There were others around her in her immediate group, colleagues from her office, all badly injured, but some still alive. No one moved. They were either limited by their injuries or trapped in fear.

She didn't know her body was suffering excruciating burns, the skin on one of her arms bubbling and falling away, likely from the jet fuel's exploding spray. The pain had yet to process. She knew only that she and a few others around her were somehow still among the living. What should they do next? How could they survive? Where to escape?

There was no way for her to know then that only a dozen people from the hundred or more in that sky lobby would make it off the floor alive.

Young sat for what she believed was ten minutes, perhaps longer, paralyzed by fear. Then she heard a voice calling out, clear and strong. Instantly she turned toward the sound. "I found the stairs," the voice said. "Follow me. Only help the ones that you can help. And follow me."

For the first time, Young stood up. There was something she heard in the man's voice, an authority, compelling her to follow. She moved toward one of her colleagues from the 86th floor who had traveled down in the group, Dianne Gladstone. Gladstone was injured and unsure she could walk. Young reached down to help as Gladstone tried to put her arms around Young. Pain burst through Young's body for the first time, leading her to realize she was badly burned. She couldn't help Gladstone up from the floor.

Young continued toward where the man had called from and, for the first time, saw him.

"It was a young man," she recalled a decade later. "Not very husky. Very short hair." She remembered he was wearing a white T-shirt and appeared to be uninjured. She thought she saw him with a red bandanna.

She paused, nodding, as if seeing the man before her right then. "That image has stuck with me," she said. "Almost on a daily basis, that image has stuck with me.

"A bunch of us just picked ourselves up and followed him right to the stairs."

Young couldn't tell how many were with her as she entered the stairwell. The smoke and dust on the floor persisted. She moved forward slowly, struggling to walk, holding her arms out in front to steady herself. Still in deep shock, the pain was there but dull, not approaching the full rage she would feel later. As she walked, she noticed a man behind her whom she described as tall and thin. She didn't know who he was. The man who steered her toward the stairwell was also with the group, walking behind her, urging her to move forward and not to stop.

They continued down the flights of stairs until the air began gradually to clear, the smoke dissipating. At one point, Young turned to see the young man behind her, the one who led her to the stairs, and for the first time she noticed he wasn't alone. He was carrying someone over his shoulder as he walked down.

"It was a very light-skinned black woman," Young recalled. "She was tall. He was holding her across his back." Young didn't know who the woman was, only that the man had apparently been carrying her the entire way down since leaving the 78th floor.

They reached what Young believed was the 61st floor, and then the man stopped. He lifted the woman from his shoulder and carefully put her down on the stairs. She sat down immediately. Young looked at the man. She remembered thinking that he had a baby face.

The man asked Young to take the fire extinguisher he'd been carrying. It looked heavy, impossible, but she lifted it. He urged her and the woman sitting on the stair to continue downward. Then he reversed course.

"I'm going back up," he said.

Young understood at once what he meant. He was going back up, seventeen flights, to the 78th floor. He was going back to the sky lobby. The man turned and, without saying another word, left her behind.

G oing back up.
   What went through his mind on the seventeen-flight climb? Every crushing breath of the ascent, each landing and turn, every foot gained and every step taken? What passed inside him each second with time disintegrating as the smoke thickened and the heat rose, as the steel melted and the jet fuel leaked? His lungs could have been failing, his strength fading.

He went back up, stepping into the fire and death, pushing through smoke and blood, bound for the sky lobby.

Why?

Maybe because he understood that if he went down, and left now, and looked away, they would be with him forever. Any of them, all of them, one of them. They were up there. He might make it down, he might rush out, he might gain the light. He might *live*.

But would they?

ing Young exhorted the woman beside her to get up and keep going down. To move even a single step at a time. The woman said she couldn't. Young left her, carrying the fire extinguisher the man had given her for a short distance, uncertain where she found the strength, before setting it down. She walked carefully, her pace slowing, until she encountered an FDNY fire marshal, Jim Devery.

Devery and fellow marshal Ron Bucca had rushed to the scene from their headquarters in Lower Manhattan after the first plane hit. Pulling up to the Trade Center, they saw the second plane fly into the face of the South Tower. They shed all thought as instinct took over. Rushing directly into the tower's lobby as the fire and smoke began to spread far above, they began making their way up the stairs. A former Green Beret and a veteran marathon runner, he was in better shape than Devery, gaining ground faster as the two climbed. Forty-six years old, Bucca would never return. People on their way down, frantic to get out, passed the two men as they ascended. Somewhere between the 40th and 50th floors, Devery saw the stairwell empty. No other civilians were coming down.

Near the 51st floor, more than 550 feet into the climb, he saw Ling Young on the stairs near the landing. She wasn't moving.

"She had her arms out. Her eyes were nearly closed, she was bleeding," Devery said. "I couldn't leave her there."

He reached out and picked up Young, carrying her as best he could down the next ten flights. Devery couldn't remember her saying anything as they climbed down. When they reached the 40th floor, exhausted, a fireman opened a door to the stairwell, asking if they needed an elevator. They left the stairs and followed the fireman into a service elevator that was still working. Seconds later, they were on the ground floor.

Devery wanted to get Young to triage, or to an ambulance, to get her medical care as soon as he could. But as he walked toward the West Street side of the building, he saw the horrible remnants of those who had leaped from the North Tower's upper floors, desperately fleeing the fire and smoke. He saw a leg still inside its red high-heeled shoe, a severed head, body parts strewn across the plaza. He took Young out a different direction, toward Vesey Street, and eventually placed her in an ambulance.

Judy Wein, the executive from Aon Corporation who saw the fireball from her window, had left her office on the 103rd floor almost immediately afterward. She too was in the sky lobby when it exploded. She was thrown through space across the floor before landing hard, her arm crushed, three ribs broken, and one of her lungs punctured.

Wein somehow made her way out, and was placed inside an ambulance with a Chinese woman. The woman was caked in dirt, bloody, and badly burned. She was clearly in shock. Wein didn't know her name. She'd never seen her before. It was Ling Young.

The ambulance carrying them pulled away. Moments later, the two women heard a fearsome roar. They turned to look out the back window.

The South Tower was falling.

. . .

Jeff was in the house alone, looking at the television.

After his brother called to tell him a plane hit the North Tower, he ran to the screen and turned it on. He fought to calm himself, to slow his heart, knowing Welles was in the South Tower. He was in a different building, separate from the images being broadcast. He was safe. He had to be. If anyone would understand how to react, it was Welles.

Then Jeff saw the second plane move across the screen and explode into the South Tower.

Almost too stunned to move, he rushed to the phone and dialed Welles's number. Busy. He tried again and again, unable to get through. When the house phone rang, it was Alison. She was hysterical. He tried to calm her down, told her not to jump to conclusions. He asked if someone else in the office could drive her home.

The doorbell rang. It was Tom Wanamaker, a local police officer and cousin of Harry Wanamaker's. Seeing him at the door, Jeff's heart nearly stopped. Why was he here? What did he know?

Tom had come straight to the house after seeing the second plane hit, to ask if Jeff had heard anything, if he'd reached Welles. No, Jeff told him. The two hugged, the officer in tears, telling Jeff he would help in any way he could. After the short visit, Wanamaker left.

Jeff returned to the room off the kitchen, to the television, transfixed by what he saw. And then, just before ten A.M., he watched the upper floors of the South Tower tilt slightly and begin to drop. Impossibly, the building began driving downward, the floors failing, the steel buckling, the structure collapsing. Seconds later, it was gone. A memory of itself, printed in dust upon the air in mammoth clouds of gray.

He stared at the screen without comprehension. The voices on television gasped at the sight, trying to recover, to offer some explanation. Jeff was already past that. He fell to his knees in the room, and cried out into the emptiness of the house. He prayed, immediately and aloud, his voice broken.

"Dear God. Take me now. Leave him here. Please. Take me."

The plea was swallowed by his weeping.

9:59 A.M. Fifty-six minutes after Flight 175 hit the South Tower.

Collapse.

The South Tower's disintegration took *ten seconds*.

Is that the time it takes to read the last three lines, to clear a dish from the table, to enter a daydream at the traffic light? To pick something to wear today, to watch a tee shot land, to address an envelope? To order off the menu, to mix a drink, to beat an egg? To lace up a shoe, to back out of the driveway, to walk out of church?

It took ten seconds for the tower's 750 million tons of heavy steel and concrete to drop, erased from the skyline, a sudden phantom. The energy released was an enormous bomb, creating dust storms and debris fields. Nearly all matter within and beneath the tower was crushed flat in those ten seconds, driven down fifty, sixty, seventy feet beneath the street. The collapse strained the bedrock below the building as it compressed cars and trucks and emergency vehicles, all absorbing the impossible weight and violence of the fall.

In the fifty-six minutes between the second plane's strike and the building's collapse, how many survived the initial moments in the impact zone and above? Who from the thirty-three highest floors escaped? Where were they now? Who was still alive?

After reaching his family as quickly as he could to let them know he was safe, Platz drifted through much of the rest of the day, unable to shake off the paralysis that so many felt, not only in the city but across the country and the world. For hours, his gaze shifted back and forth between the images playing on the television and the smoke from downtown drifting outside the bedroom windows. The calls he made went unanswered, the door to the apartment stayed shut.

As night fell, he left the apartment and went to the only place he could think of, guided as much by routine as by the hopeful message he'd left earlier in the morning.

He sat in the bar at Boxers for hours. Every time he heard the door open, he looked to see if it was Welles. Finally the owner, offering his apologies, said he needed to leave. It was time to close.

Night came. No word. Nothing.

Welles's parents and sisters, aunts and uncles, college buddies and teammates, fellow firefighters and childhood friends, all the circles of his life, yearned to sustain hope, to find encouragement where they could.

Kevin Tiernan, a friend of Welles's since childhood who the night before had been with him watching *Monday Night Football,* found the wait intolerable. He was one of the thousands who searched Manhattan's hospitals one by one, making a desperate tour and finding the emergency rooms gravely still, awaiting the rush that never came.

Jeff and Alison could hardly remember all the visitors and prayers and plates of ziti. They answered as many calls as they could stand before letting others answer, accepting the hopes, passing each of them along. The same vigil, held to the glow of television sets and the hum of news accounts, was playing out in thousands of other houses as well.

They all waited, some steadfast and others stripped, holding back their grief.

The next day, Wednesday, Chuck Platz breathed deeply, paused, and walked into Welles's bedroom for the first time.

Platz was twenty-three years old. The most significant loss he'd experienced in his life was the death of his grandfather when he was seven years old. No one else he'd known well had died.

He looked down at the threshold, the saddle of wood on the floor between the hallway and the room. He paused.

Outside, where streets had been blocked off and an emergency force mobilized, where a smoldering pile complicated by bodies rose 150 feet in the air, where the small city of the Twin Towers had populated the sky a day before, where families and friends were beginning to post signs of their missing loved ones on every flat surface they could find, where a city ever boastful of its imperviousness and its clout had been pierced and its psyche shaken, outside there were millions of souls all grappling, alone and together, with anger and pain, doubt and fear.

Inside apartment 19, there was stillness where yesterday there was luminous motion. The room was proof. Silent. Implacable.

The glass of water was still on the dresser.

The dry cleaning receipts for his suits were still pinned underneath a wooden loon, the one he used as a paperweight.

The dent from Welles's head was still there in the pillow.

In the silence, Platz heard the first echoes of his friend's life. Nothing definite had emerged as to his fate, no authority had decreed his end, no official had called or come by. But in his heart, Platz understood. He knew. He was not beyond denial, but he had occupied the same space and breathed the same air his friend did the day before. That held more than proximity. The space contained a truth.

He could hear Welles walking out the door, the sound forever tracked in his mind. The vacancy of Welles's room would stay with him for years to come.

"Even today, I take a second to look around my room when I'm leaving for the day," he said more than a decade later. "To maybe tidy up the bed or clean things up. Not that I'm thinking I'm not coming back, but it's just this little reminder, in the back of my head, of what it was like to walk into his room, of what it looked like, just the way it was when he walked out the door that day.

"I find myself doing little things like closing the closet door, fixing up the bed, putting the remote on the back table. . . . I feel like I'm doing them because of the memory of walking into his room and seeing it like he just left it. He left as if he was coming back. . . . It was hard to see. So I think maybe in some ways, I try to make it look neat when I leave my place. For him."

eff was the one who went to the city to search, to fill out the forms and answer the questions, to engage with the official machinery of loss. The morning after the attacks, he woke up early to make the ride in with his friend Tom Weekley. Jeff brought Welles's New York State pistol permit with him, for the fingerprints it contained. He also went to the family dentist, without being asked, to collect his son's dental records.

He joined a march of loved ones bearing the open wounds of their panic. Maybe it was natural that families of the missing turned here, to a place meant to symbolize security. They came to a fortress in the city.

The armory on Lexington Avenue and Twenty-sixth Street, on the East Side of Manhattan, was the headquarters of the New York National Guard First Battalion, Sixty-ninth Infantry Regiment. The families and friends of those who worked at the World Trade Center and had yet to return home came to the armory to file missing-persons reports. The hope was to match a name to a face of a very small number of the wounded being treated at city hospitals, those without any clear identification. The building was designated as a family assistance center, and it drew everyone still holding out hope.

The families arrived early. They refused to be mourners, not yet. In lines snaking around the entire block, they carried evidence of their love, and proofs of identity. There were pictures and letters, medical records and physical descriptions. Hundreds carried flyers advertising their missing, lives whittled down to the physical facts of being: name, age, height, weight, topped by a single picture. Nearly all the flyers ended with a list of phone numbers to call.

The notices were placed everywhere: on telephone poles and mailboxes, on streetlamps and tree trunks. They formed a pleading and dense collage on the walls of the armory itself.

Jeff came with proofs and markers of his son's life, to join the somber line of those waiting to file reports and submit to police interviews. Years later, he'd recall nearby residents who came out of their apartment buildings with sandwiches and cookies to offer, a way to try to comfort those touched most by the assault on their city. The memory would bring tears to his eyes.

After speaking with two NYPD detectives and providing all the information he could, he left the armory. To the south, smoke from the pile stained the sky. In inaccessible pockets far below the ground, the fires would burn for months to come.

Thursday morning. Two days. Nearly fifty hours.

Each was a universe unto itself, vast and empty.

At 10:45 A.M., the doorbell rang. Jeff was in the city, covering the terrain as best he could there. Alison was home, exhausted with worry, when she heard it.

She walked to the door and saw Harry Wanamaker standing outside, covered in silt, ash soaked into the fiber of his gear and caked on his turnouts. Wanamaker stood with his helmet under his arm, his eyes straight upon her. He'd come directly from the scorched ground of the Trade Center complex, where he'd spent every moment not spent on Marine 1's fireboats, throwing himself into the ruins of the pile. The only stop he made before coming to the house on Birchwood was at his own, to take off his boots and put on clean socks. He didn't want to track dirt across her floor.

Less than three months before, on a June night, he'd stood on the deck of his fireboat surrounded by his friends from Empire Hook and Ladder. He had toured them around Lower Manhattan, and stood next to Welles, arm to arm, with the Twin Towers behind them, soaring and dark. He was relaxed, the collar of his blue shirt open, a smile creasing his face, Welles's own grin wide beside him.

Now Harry stood outside the door looking at Welles's mother, his face drawn and exhausted. Alison's breath caught at the sight of him. She opened the door and ushered him in.

"Harry," she said. "My God . . . what are you doing here?"

"I've just come back," he said.

"Let me get you in here, and get you some food."

He walked inside. "I just want to tell you . . . we're doing everything we can."

It wasn't the prayer answered. It wasn't her child delivered. But he wanted her to know he would make every effort, and everyone else would too. They would do everything they could do.

They sat and talked for an hour, Harry trying to eat the lunch she quickly made for him. There was everything to say, and nothing. He tried to explain the collapse of the buildings, the unthinkable scope of the ruins, the way the fireboat rushed to the scene upon receiving the first call. But over and over, Harry said the same words in a fragment or a sentence, a pledge and a wish. He gave them voice to make them real. He said it, so together they might believe it.

"We're going to find him."

Very early Friday morning, long before dawn, Alison was back at her task. The girls were sleeping, she hoped. Her job was to call the city's hospitals and emergency rooms searching for someone not yet identified, to see if a voice might pick up the line, take the information, deliver the miracle. To hear a nurse or doctor rush back, out of breath and ecstatic, to exclaim, *Yes, yes, he's here. He fits that description. He answers to that name. He's yours. He's found.*

Getting someone to answer was nearly impossible no matter

how many times she dialed, to the point where her fingers grew numb. She knew she was one of thousands making these calls, from kitchens and living rooms, offices and dens, in desperation.

She began to call late, the hours on either side of midnight, and all through the dawn. She'd call from the room downstairs, so as not to disturb the girls and to let Jeff find any traces of sleep that he could. It was nearly three days since the attacks. She stood up from the desk to stretch and walk around the room a few paces, to get away from the mute hammer of the receiver and gather the energy for the next call.

That's when she felt him. In the room.

"His presence," she said. It was more than a vision. There was an energy there, a vital field reaching out to her. She wanted to turn around from the desk and look behind her, toward the dark right corner of the room, but she didn't. To turn and look would be, in her mind, a lack of faith in him. The house was otherwise still and dim. She'd had visions before. This was different. It was not a clear sight, it was a connection, a communication.

"I just knew it was Welles," she said. "I knew."

She didn't hesitate or startle. She spoke directly into the space before her.

"Welles," she said his name. She waited, but not long. She wanted to acknowledge him. She said the first words inside her.

"Thank you." She wanted him to know what this gave to her, what the moment contained. She had the phone message he'd left, she could hear the voice and perhaps already knew how she would play it, to hold the sound of him near. The feeling in the room now was different, a force more than a sound.

"If you can do that," she said, referring to the energy and the field and the feeling, to the connection, "I know you're okay. You're not here anymore."

It was around three A.M. She continued to look straight ahead, her back to the presence.

"I know you're okay," she said.

She stood for several long moments as the presence receded, leaving her alone in the silence of the house.

She made a decision, a silent step. Looking at the phone, she turned away. "That's when I gave up looking," she said. "Because I knew he was gone."

The winds blew gently through the Hudson Valley, rippling the waters, stirring the trees. The final Saturday in September was cool, the promise of autumn deepening, as they gathered, carrying their emptiness inside.

Light poured through the stained-glass window, rounded and majestic, filling the sanctuary with soft beams from above the arched wooden doors.

Grace Episcopal Church in Nyack, a century and a half old, stood in its place on First Avenue, its massive stone façade stern and comforting. It was the Crowther family's church even before moving to town, a place of worship and fellowship, of community and solidarity.

On this day, September 29, 2001, it was a place to say good-bye.

More than a thousand came, filling the sanctuary's space, with more waiting outside in brilliant sunshine. The church drew them together as the central point in so many circles of Welles's life. They arrived to pay tribute, and to mourn.

The Reverend Richard Gressle, the church's rector, spoke in Scripture and used the words of Christ. He challenged those gathered to embrace their sorrow, but also to look beyond it, as an example and a standard by which to live.

"Welles, who befriended the world, has taken that step beyond," he said. "It is our responsibility that we honor who he was by befriending one another and the world."

For so many inside, especially those closest to the altar, sitting in the first few rows, the world felt different now, smaller, harder, reduced. Its horizon had collapsed; the views across the water were empty.

Welles's sister Honor, two years younger, delivered the eulogy. She stood at the front of the church, looking out at her parents and sister, her aunts and uncles, and the rows of pews behind them, filled and silent, save for the sobbing and the echo of her own voice. The decision to have the memorial service was complicated, only arriving over time as the first few weeks passed and hope made its slow turn to grief. If it was surrender, no one would say. Acceptance was far off, in some unmarked distance.

She spoke with heart and humor, describing not a saint but a brother—in terms real and warm, the bond laid bare for all to hear and feel. On September 11, driving with her boyfriend, Rick, from their apartment in Mount Kisco to her parents' house, she was filled with a terrible sense of certainty. She knew, even before reaching Nyack, that her brother was gone. She would fight to keep hope, but as they crossed the Hudson, she heard his voice come to her, Welles speaking to her, her feeling him. The message was clear. She should be the one to speak for him. Whenever the moment came, it should be her. And she made another decision on that drive. Still single, in her first year of law school at St. John's, Honor knew that she would name her first child after her brother. As soon as she arrived home, she began composing lines in her mind, many she would say now. She felt the words came from them both, mingled. She was the Tonto to his Lone Ranger, the Watson to his Sherlock Holmes. She recalled the bright times and the sibling fights, the lacrosse practices and the training runs. They were part of daily life, and they would live on in memory.

"He helped me understand our bumps and bruises were badges of courage," she said, looking out at the assembly in its black and muted dress.

"His ability to laugh led him to see the best in any situation. . . . He could brighten a room from the house next door." It was courageous and honest and real. It didn't set her brother upon a pedestal, but cast him as a boy, and then a man, who stood beside her as they each grew every day until he was gone.

After she finished, others followed. Friends of Welles's laughed and wept, their numbness thawing if only for an hour or two, opening themselves to receive his absence now as something final.

Near the end of the memorial service, Jeff watched as Bill Cassidy, Empire Hook and Ladder's company chaplain and for the entire Nyack Fire Department as well, walked to the front of the church. Jeff had been the company chaplain once too, and had stood where Cassidy was now. He had delivered the words he was now about to hear, in tribute to other fallen firefighters. All those services had been for men much older. None had been for his son.

Cassidy recited an order of the service Jeff had shared many times before.

The last alarm has sounded for our brother.
To Welles has come that last call.
It is the call from which there is no turning away,
The imperative and final order,
Of the great chief and captain of us all . . .

The words rang through the church.

Jeff's brother Bosley gave the final reading, straining with emotion, delivering lines from Tennyson's elegy "Crossing the Bar."

The remarks done, the echoes quieted, mourners stood and turned to leave. Alison walked from the pew and saw the doors open, flooding the entire space with a dazzling light. The world beyond the church's threshold was difficult to glimpse, its reality blank and flat. But as she got closer to the exit, she began to discern figures standing along the sidewalk, lining the entire frontage of the church lot. There was a color guard and an honor guard, and there were firefighters as far as she could see, standing in uniform dress. They stood still and solemn, flanking the ladder truck from Empire Hook and Ladder No. 1.

The sight overwhelmed her and her body buckled before Jeff caught her. She beheld the large American flag flying from the truck, rolling with the breezes off the river. It was placed prominently, proudly.

There was no casket over which to drape it.

III

AS A CREEPING DARKNESS IT MOVES, SET OUT FROM *its launch unseen, at a time unknown. And then it's in you, with each dawn, a shadow in every light.*

Its force is inevitable and, somehow, still surprising. We know we will feel it, as surely as we know our names and hold our loved ones and count our days. We know we will bear its weight. But before it arrives, we know it only as abstraction, a dim light in the fog across the river, an echo of the train's roar. Only when it lands and we feel the awful mass of vacancy do we understand how unready we are.

As a plague, a hollowing out, it insinuates itself—a suffering that can never be approximated, no matter how many others we see enduring it.

That's its onslaught, more complete and consuming than we might ever expect, swallowing us—not from top down, but from last breath to next. The death of a child before the parents, the fracturing of life's cycle, the interruption of generations. A permanent emptiness.

It is more profound than terror. Terror fades.
Grief lasts.

For many weeks, she couldn't look at his picture.

She couldn't bear the sight of his face. While others carried pictures of their lost, in large frames or folded flyers or in their wallets or purses, always at the ready, she avoided the image of her son.

"I couldn't look him in the eye," Alison said. "I couldn't face him."

The intensity of her love and the promise of his life were unbearable to contemplate. The picture represented not just a moment in time, but time stopped. There would be no more frames to add.

He was twenty-four. Those were hours in a day, not years in a life. Not a quarter century reached, not a woman courted and married, no children expected and born, no family of his own to love and raise. He would never have them. The deepest, richest parts of his life, the challenges accepted and rewards gained, the sunsets over the river and the trips back home, the gifts opened and the failures absorbed, all of it interrupted, stopped.

She had pictures. She wouldn't look at them. Not yet.

For the first few months, nearly every time she stepped outside the front door, she was unable to return without friends and neighbors offering an embrace or a gesture of comfort. All of it was well meaning, but also exhausting and emptying. There was nowhere in town to go without all who saw her knowing whom she had lost, and how she'd lost him. Alison would end up comforting others who were trying to help her.

As the holidays approached, she felt herself needing to escape, and she took a job for a couple of months in retail, working at the upscale department store Neiman Marcus across the river in White Plains. She went to work, finding a context where strangers sought nothing from her beyond a transaction. She wanted to be seen but not watched, to be heard but not known.

The holidays were excruciating. Paige and Honor gave her a pair of earrings, telling her they were from Welles, the gesture accompanied by kindness and torment, the pain incessant. "I cried," Alison said. "Hard. Every day, at some point of the day, I just cried."

The sorrow was damaging, wearing her away.

At some point, her friend and neighbor Fran Sennas, Stacey Sennas McGowan's mother, visited the house. As a managing director at Sandler, Stacey helped Welles, a fellow Nyack High School and Boston College alum. She opened the door for his first summer internship, and, ultimately, to land the job with the firm. Without her help, he might never have worked at the Trade Center. Thirty-eight years old, married with two young daughters, four and five years old, she also died in the attacks.

Fran brought over a bottle of holy water a friend had given her, drawn from the sacred spring in Lourdes, France, where pilgrims had traveled for centuries with the faith that the water might cure all afflictions. Alison accepted the gift from Fran, each woman walking her own path through the emptiness and anguish. She looked at the bottle, then drew it to her lips and took a small sip.

"After that," Alison said, "I stopped crying."

The pain didn't stop. The door didn't swing open. The phone didn't ring. But something entered her. "It just brought me a peace," she said.

It didn't bring answers as to where he lay, or what he'd done before the tower fell, but day and night in the pit of ground zero, in the twisted ruins, hundreds were working, clearing, digging. They were getting closer to the bottom.

They needed Welles to be found, and returned. They understood that this was a search that could end only in ritual, but the ritual mattered.

As devastating as the loss was, there was a deeper cry in its ache. He was not only gone. He was lost. There was a difference. While his absence was a fact in every instant of the day, the longing to bring him back home was a separate anguish—a feeling that he'd been abandoned, by his family and the world, left in a place somehow colder than death.

Port Authority Police Lieutenant John Ryan was among those who came to work day after day, month after month, in the hollow of that place. From the day he arrived at the World Trade Center on September 11, he would be a part of the tireless militia of recovery, the group of people who devoted themselves to sifting through the pile, and to retrieving the bodies and remains buried within it.

As commander of the Port Authority Police Department's rescue and recovery operation at ground zero, Ryan understood the feelings of the families. They were close to his own. While there was much attention on the loss of 343 members of the FDNY, the PAPD had suffered as well, losing 37 officers in the attacks. Ryan felt deeply connected to, and responsible for, all of them. To work in the pile forced a choice—a hardening and closing off of one's heart, or a daily and ferocious fight to keep it open, against the horrors of the task. Ryan fought each day with every recovery.

"We would place the remains in a body bag," he said. "We would drape it with an American flag. We would perform an honor guard and carry the remains to a temporary morgue site."

Initially, the custom was reserved for members of the departments only, those recovered with clear identifications, either their police shields or the markings of the FDNY's gear. But in time, Ryan instituted a change. He wasn't sure exactly when, but he was present when a set of remains was found, the body in an FDNY T-shirt. The understanding on the pile was to let each department retrieve its own. When Ryan reached out to a counterpart with the fire department, he was told that anyone could buy a T-shirt, that there needed to be more proof for the honor guard and flag to be used. Ryan disagreed. He came to the belief that all who perished on the site, in uniform or not, serving a designated department or working as a civilian, shared the same hallowed ground and should be united in their most basic designation. The distinctions, to him, were wrong.

"Every set of remains," he said, "would be wrapped in an American flag, and with the honor guard. I didn't need to know who the person was that we were recovering. . . . At that point I changed it." Every recovery was treated with the same due ceremony.

Alison picked up the violin, surprised by its strangeness in her hands, its foreign weight and feel. For the first time in nearly twenty years, she played again. In a different life, almost all of it in the open country before children, she played every day. Alison had been a concert-level violinist, a passion that ran deep inside her. It was never the only pursuit in her life, but there was something in its discipline and purity that spoke to her, its demands and rewards an inarguable equation. Then came marriage, and then came Welles and the girls. The violin came out of her hands to be put in its case. Welles remembered her playing in a concert.

It was a Tuesday, March 19, 2002. Half a year had passed. Two days before, at the start of the week, Alison had been watching the news at home, her hunger for information never sated. By this time, much of the compacted debris of the pile at ground zero had been cleared. A last major area remained, near an access road built within the acreage of the gaping hole. For those who worked at the pile, and for the victims' families especially, it was an anxious time, a fear deepening that they would never receive their loved ones' remains. Much of the pile was gone.

The news report stated that excavation would begin in the area underneath the central ramp leading down into the pit. Without knowing the exact geography, Alison was still struck by the report. She sensed that maybe this was the place where Welles would be. She'd learned not to hold back from such feelings. To keep them inside would be to collapse from their weight. Whatever she felt, she acknowledged and accepted. She gave the feelings voice, most often to the person closest, to Jeff.

She looked at him after hearing the report and without hesitation made a declaration she'd never made before.

"Jeff," she said. "They're going to find Welles. This week. They're going to find him."

He looked at her, hearing her certainty, even if he didn't share the same expectation. Of course he wanted his son back, in the most desperate way. But he didn't make these declarations the way Alison did.

"Well, okay," he said, accepting her belief.

It wasn't the only feeling she'd had in the week. In truth, she'd picked up the violin spurred by something more than restlessness. That Tuesday, Alison took a lesson with her friend Ed Simons, the music director and conductor of the Rockland County Symphony Orchestra. She could read music as well as ever, but the translation by her hands was lacking. Her fingers were still unused to the bending and positioning. Simons, who'd conducted her for years, was patient and encouraging. But it was the memory of Welles's encouragement that brought her to try again.

Last summer, without any cue that she could recall, he had told her as much.

"Mom, you should start playing again," he said. "Just start." This was the week when she did.

The lesson with Simons was in Pomona, near the house where they lived when Welles was born, before the family moved to Upper Nyack. Afterward, she drove past the old house and parked, spending time looking out and looking back.

"I just had this wonderful warmth," Alison said. "Welles was really with me, really close."

Three days later, the Friday of that same week, March 22, Alison was with her youngest daughter, Paige, accompanying her on a visit to the State University of New York in nearby Purchase. SUNY Purchase was a magnet for aspiring artists, with one of the strongest performing arts programs in the country. Paige, an elite dancer considering a life in professional ballet, was auditioning for the university's dance conservatory.

Alison was reading, waiting, when Paige joined her during a break. A few minutes later, her cell phone rang. It was a house-keeper calling.

"There's a policeman here, at the door," she said.

Alison wondered if one of the family's dogs had gotten loose and was marauding through the neighborhood.

The policeman came on the line. "Mrs. Crowther," he said. In the tone of those two words, she knew it was something else entirely. She stepped away from Paige, the phone to her ear.

"Mrs. Crowther," the voice said, "your son's body has been recovered at ground zero."

She fought desperately not to cry. Trying to collect herself, she thought of Paige and her audition, not wanting to cast any shade over her daughter, who'd suffered in her own way through these long months. She didn't want to take an ounce of light from her daughter's day, but how not to? She brought herself back to the phone in her hand, and found courage enough to ask the question. "How did they identify him?"

"By his fingerprints."

"His fingerprints? Oh my God . . ."

It was certain. It was her son.

The call ended. She stood there, overwhelmed, but determined to be present for Paige. To support her daughter in her moment as best she could. Her mind had to slow. There would be procedures to follow and forms to sign and documents to examine.

Later in the day, Paige sensed that something had happened, and she asked her mother what was wrong. Alison could hold it no longer. She looked at her daughter.

"They found Welles," she said.

T he remains were found three days before the family was notified, the time necessary for the body to be transported from ground zero, taken for examination, and ultimately identified.

The date of Welles's recovery, Tuesday, March 19, brought an odd measure of comfort. Their first child was born on a Tuesday. He died on a Tuesday. On a Tuesday, he was found. And, of course, on the nineteenth, his number in all things since his boyhood, chosen for nearly every jersey he wore, even down to the apartment number he shared with Chuck Platz in the city.

Alison and Jeff still had a hard trip to the city's chief medical examiner's office on East Twenty-sixth Street. It was the place where death was made official, and where its cause, manner, and mechanism were determined for the entire jurisdiction of New York City. The loss of life at the World Trade Center was the most profound challenge the office had ever faced, both in scale and in level of scrutiny. The examiners were called to the site to begin the process of identification almost immediately. As the months passed, the natural process of decay affected even those relatively few bodies that had somehow remained largely whole through the devastation. Most, of course, were in pieces.

In the first ten months after the attacks, the office identified more than twelve hundred victims at ground zero. A much smaller number, fewer than three hundred, were discovered intact, or nearly so.

Jeff and Alison came to the Manhattan office to find out as much as they could about their son's end, or at least as much as they could bear. How many details could they endure, how many facts could they accept, beyond the final one?

Together, they passed into the offices, with its motto written on the lobby wall: "Science Serving Justice."

They met with a medical examiner and asked their first question: What condition was he in when recovered?

Part of his lower right jaw was missing. As was his right hand. Beyond that, the rest of the body was largely intact.

Where was he found?

The body was recovered in the debris of what had been the lobby of the South Tower.

For Jeff and Alison, this answer was a revelation.

The lobby. Could that really be? From 104 floors above, when the second plane struck, all the way down to the ground?

Somehow, some way, he had made it down.

How? How close was he to getting out? To surviving? Could he have made it? Why didn't he? What stopped him? What was he doing? Who was he with?

Jeff felt the answer immediately, even as so many other questions flooded through his mind: *He was helping.*

They learned more. Welles's body was found that March in an area of the pit where firefighters' remains were recovered. Most specifically, he lay close to FDNY assistant chief Donald Burns. Burns, sixty-one, one of the most respected members of the entire department, had been a responding commander during the 1993 attack at the World Trade Center in the North Tower, decorated many times over in his thirty-nine years serving. As a citywide commander, he covered all major incidents and emergencies across the five boroughs. As the chief in charge of the South Tower on September 11, he had set up a command post in the tower lobby, helping to lead the evacuation effort for thousands who survived, as well as to guide the department's responding personnel through the challenge of fighting a raging fire nearly a quarter mile up in the sky. Burns's body was discovered in an area of rubble beside the remains of ten other firefighters. And those of Welles Crowther.

John Ryan, the commander of the Port Authority Police Department's rescue and recovery operation at ground zero, who covered the pile from that September day all the way through the following spring, knew every inch of the tower lobby down to the tile. He was familiar with the area where the command post had been set up that morning, and the debris field where Burns, Welles, and others were recovered.

"The command post location was selected," Ryan said, "so that responders coming in from the street would be able to go to it with relative ease."

He understood what that meant for the families of those recovered in or near that spot: they were close to making it out of the building, to the safety of the street, to the rest of their lives.

He estimated the distance to the exits at seventy-five feet.

"People found in that area," Ryan said, "were seconds away from being clear."

To be so close to an escape but to remain inside was not coincidence. Likely, it was a choice. Welles made it. He *was* helping.

He was at work.

There was now a body, so there would be a service.

Not in the brilliant September sunshine, but on a gray March day, at Hannemann Funeral Home in Nyack, where Welles was being prepared for cremation, and then at Grace Church, where his ashes would later be immured. For now, his family stood beside him, waiting.

Jeff and Alison were there, beside Honor and her boyfriend, Rick, the man she loved and would later marry. Paige was there too, with Amy Rappaport, a lifelong friend. Welles's remains were wrapped in an American flag, resting in a plain wooden box, humbler, lesser than a coffin. It's a moment, and a sight, Paige has never forgotten.

"I remember thinking to myself," she said, "my big brother fits in that small box. The box was too small for him . . ." She paused, crying at the memory. "It was not substantial enough for my big brother and his big personality and his big size. It just seemed like a box that a four-foot child could fit in . . ."

The Reverend Richard Gressle, who had presided over the memorial service at Grace Church back in the fall, joined the family, along with the funeral director and staff. They were there to receive Welles, pray over him, and send him onward. Not the thousand mourners who gathered back in September, not the public farewell. He lay now in the close grip of family.

Neither Jeff nor Alison had seen Welles without covering since he was found. Jeff asked the director of the funeral home about the condition of the body, and whether he should see him. The answer was short and definitive.

"Jeff, no," he was told. "You don't want that."

He understood.

As the group prepared to take Welles to the crematorium, there was a point when Alison stood next to her son's remains, looking down upon the flag, the box open. She had carried the water from Lourdes with her in a bottle. She reached toward the flag's edge. Jeff and the funeral director saw her and both reacted quickly, to keep her from lifting its edge any higher, to block her from seeing what lay beneath. But that wasn't her intent. She had no desire for such an image to supplant the ones she carried with her. She reached for the flag with one hand, and with the other she lifted the bottle and poured the water out gently, the fabric darkening as it absorbed the drops. She watched as the dampness seeped into the form beneath.

"I poured it all over him," she said, thinking back to the moment, "in the hopes of somehow bringing him back to life again. And I knew in my heart, a part of me knew that it wouldn't be possible really. But I just had to do that.

"And sure enough, he did come back to life, when his story came out."

On Sunday of Memorial Day weekend, 2002, the *New York Times* landed on the Crowthers' doorstep in the morning, as it always did.

There was an understanding in the Crowther house that Jeff read the paper first. He liked to go through the Sunday *Times* in a certain order.

In the months since September, newspaper stories about the terrorist attacks remained a staple, but they came with less frequency now. The city was trying to find its way through recovery, even as the hole in Lower Manhattan remained a gaping wound. Alison was still gripped by every story, but Jeff had a different reaction. For the most part, he turned the page, the reminder painful and unwelcome. The sadness was challenge enough without the news adding to it.

Jeff opened the paper that morning and saw a feature piece on the front page with the large headline FIGHTING TO LIVE AS THE TOWERS DIED.

The story, written by *Times* reporters Jim Dwyer, Eric Lipton, Kevin Flynn, James Glanz, and Ford Fessenden, was several thousand words long. It would become the basis for the seminal book *102 Minutes,* written by Dwyer and Flynn, a comprehensive and masterful chronicle of reporting and writing documenting the space of time between the first plane strike and the second tower's collapse, filled with direct accounts from survivors as well as dispatches from the families, colleagues, and friends of those lost. The book would become the definitive account of the fight for survival as the buildings burned and then fell.

As much respect as Jeff had for the *Times* and its deep connections to his father, he knew right away that he wouldn't read the piece. By this point, more than eight months after Welles's death, his reaction was nearly reflexive. He also knew that Alison would want to scan every word.

"Alison," he called to her. "There's an article in the paper here. You may want to see this."

She saw the headline, took the front section of the paper, and went to their bedroom. Atop the bed, she sat up and began reading through the minute-by-minute account of what was happening in the towers as the attacks unfolded. For all the information she'd digested already, all the reports she'd consumed in print and on air, she'd never read anything like this. The detail was breathtaking, heartbreaking. The piece placed her inside the buildings, side by side with survivors and victims.

She began to read the accounts of those on the 78th floor of the South Tower, the sky lobby, where Flight 175's lower wing exploded into the building, slashing through the crowd waiting for the elevators. She read of the obliterating intensity of the impact, of the instant wave of death, but also of several who somehow survived the plane's strike. Her mind stopped for a moment, going back to the phone message Welles left her. The time. With the chronology provided so clearly in the article, laid out for her more plainly than she'd ever seen before, she reconsidered the timing of Welles's day.

He'd left the message for her after the plane hit the South Tower, as lives vanished and catastrophe deepened. Alison knew that his remains had been found in the ruins of the ground-floor lobby. She began to imagine his path down from the 104th floor on the stairs, and likely his coming upon the distress and terror of the sky lobby. She believed that if he saw any part of it, any of the devastation depicted so vividly in the article, there would be no way for him to pass by. He'd respond. That was his training. That was her son.

And that's when she read it. Two thirds of the way through the long piece. In the 128th paragraph of the story. She stopped, staring at the two sentences:

> *A mysterious man appeared at one point, his mouth and nose covered with a red handkerchief. He was looking for a fire extinguisher.*

She was gripped by the three simple words, the five syllables, black type on off-white paper, looming before her.

A red handkerchief.

Jeff was in the kitchen, deprived of the front section of the paper and taking refuge in the Sunday crossword, when he heard Alison shout.

"Jeff! Jeff! Get in here!"

He came rushing to the bedroom, where Alison had the paper open in front of her.

"I found Welles," she said, and then repeated it, so it might sink into them both. She read aloud the portion of the article, and pointed to the description of the mysterious man in the ruins and fires of the 78th-floor sky lobby, his face covered with the red cloth.

Jeff tried to be measured, calm, in the face of Alison's excitement. Before he could answer, she broke in.

"That has to be Welles," she said. "That's where he would've been, the 78th floor, that sky lobby. With the bandanna."

"No," Jeff replied, as evenly as he could. "We don't know that. We don't know that's him. It could've been anyone else there."

"Maybe," Alison acknowledged. "I know we don't know if it's him. But I know. I know it's him."

Thanks to the *Times*'s reporting, she also knew the names of two survivors who mentioned seeing the mysterious man and his red handkerchief, a man they saw trying to lead others to safety. The survivors were among the eighteen in or above the plane's impact zone who miraculously made it out. Their names were completely foreign to Alison in the moment, but the introduction was there, in stark print. Ling Young and Judy Wein.

Alison was going to find them.

Not finding a clear lead for Ling Young in the *Times* article, Alison focused initially on Judy Wein, listed in the piece as working for Aon Corporation, on the 103rd floor of the South Tower. She called Aon first.

"Judy isn't here," came the reply.

Alison tried to explain the nature of her inquiry, but how? The company lost scores of its employees in the attacks, every victim with a family who wanted to know about those final hours, about where he was, how she fought, what they felt. How could she press into that wound for her own answers?

Alison mentioned what she'd read in the *Times,* and asked if there was any way the office might pass on her contact information. She told the receptionist she might know who helped to save Judy Wein, and she needed to talk to her. The receptionist took down her information and the call ended.

Later that day, Wein called back. In the aftermath of her escape, she'd shared every detail with her husband, Gerry Sussman, from her hospital bed. From then forward, Gerry became an integral part of telling her story. While Judy spoke to the *Times'*s Eric Lipton, giving her account of survival directly to the reporter, the interview was in fact a rarity. Despite the onslaught of media requests and inquiries that came asking her to share her story, Judy rarely granted interviews. Gerry handled nearly all the requests, and when Judy agreed to cooperate, primarily it was Gerry who served as the intermediary, as the voice for Judy's experience, speaking for her in interviews. In nearly all cases, that was the arrangement. According to Gerry, Judy had a deep, personal motivation for giving the *Times* interview directly.

"She was hoping that they would uncover the man with the red handkerchief." The *Times* story set the search in motion.

Judy listened as Alison described some of the simplest facts about Welles. She was trying not to overload Judy or pressure her into any kind of confirmation. She could hear Jeff's voice in her head, urging caution and the proper dose of uncertainty. She told herself she was prepared to hear what she hoped not to: that it wasn't him. But she needed to know one way or the other. Not to pursue an answer, an identification, would be a different kind of abandonment. She couldn't live with herself if she didn't try.

Would Judy say the man was African American, or in his forties or fifties, or heavy, or had a visible tattoo or scar . . . no to each one. The possibility was still alive with each answer. As Judy remembered, the man was white, young, fit, as best she could tell. Alison felt herself getting closer to the answer, but was not there yet.

"I think it may have been my son who saved you," Alison said on the phone. "He was always carrying a red bandanna with him, even in his business suit. He was a trained firefighter. From what I read, I just . . . I believe it was him."

The red bandanna was fixed in Judy's mind and vision. She wanted to know the man's identity too, of course, to know who had emerged from the smoke to lead her to safety. Though if this was the man, the identification would also carry a sad truth.

She could never thank him.

On the call, Judy told Alison there was an e-mail chain connecting a group of South Tower survivors, the few who'd made it out from the 78th-floor sky lobby or above. She and Gerry would send the inquiry down the line, to see who might have seen the man, if anyone else spotted a red bandanna. Then Alison asked a simple question:

"Can I send you a picture of my son?"

Alison got the address, looked for a recent photo, and sent it out overnight. As soon as the envelope left her hand, the wait began.

Judy Wein looked at the photo that spilled from the envelope, a picture of Welles from his Boston College graduation, taken in the spring of 1999, a little more than two years before September 11. He was smiling, proud, facing into the future.

Gerry recalled his wife's reaction, and her response.

"Although it was dark and smoky and hard to see very clearly in the sky lobby," Gerry said, "Judy did get a clear picture of Welles after he brought her into the well-lit stairwell. He wasn't wearing the red handkerchief then. And there she saw him. She remembered what he looked like.

"And she identified him," Gerry said. His wife was clear, without doubt, certain. She knew.

"Yes," she told her husband, "that was the man."

Gerry paused a moment in his recollection.

"It was very sad," he said. "Until that time we really didn't know if he'd survived."

. . .

To be certain, Judy and Gerry sent the photo of Welles out through the survivors' group e-mail chain. Was there anyone else who escaped the building who remembered seeing this man in the picture and could identify him as the one who led the way out of the sky lobby, into Stairway A, and down?

Judy knew two others, Gigi Singer and Ed Nicholls, both injured in the impact, who were close behind her as she made her way to the stairwell and began the descent. She didn't know who else had been guided to the stairs by the man with the red bandanna. She knew Singer and Nicholls might not have seen the man, but both followed her after she heard the man's instructions. Likely, none of them would've found the way without his guiding them. That's what she told her husband.

"The people who went down with Judy," he said, "were actually saved by Welles, although they may not realize that. I don't know how they actually got into the stairwell, but certainly Judy was the first one in and then these people followed, and they went down the stairs with Judy."

After the photo went out, a reply came quickly, not from a survivor but from one of her children. Richard Young, Ling Young's son, saw the e-mail and wondered if this was the man his mother had told him about from the beginning, the man who walked with her down the stairs.

Since making it down, Ling had been consumed by the struggle to recover. The mental trauma endured, playing out in scenes that couldn't be blocked, images from the sky lobby in its first moments after the plane struck. Her physical recovery was a different trial, the inferno living on inside her in the excruciating pain of her wounds and the endless hospital visits. The second- and third-degree burns covered more than a quarter of her body. For the first five weeks after the attacks, she never stepped foot from the hospital.

"I was not just burned," Ling said. "They were thermal burns, which means . . . I was cooked." She looked down at the scars on her arm. "I had a lot of complications, lot of infections. No matter what they did, my skin grafts didn't work."

By June, she'd already endured six surgeries—each its own torment, and all exhausting. With every procedure she saw her recovery time expanding, a road with no apparent end. Still, when Ling's mind flashed back to the furnace of the 78th floor, to the scores of dead and dying surrounding her, she also couldn't help but wonder about the man who emerged from the flames, who spoke with such authority, who steered her way and guided her down. She'd never seen him again. Did he make it out? How did he know what to do? Would they ever meet? What would she say to thank him?

Richard asked his mother the question: "Doesn't this sound like the man who took you down?"

It did, but she wasn't sure. Judy's story was different from hers. Judy stressed the sight of the handkerchief, the red bandanna, across the rescuer's face. It was the most significant image of her rescuer, at least as Ling read it. Ling had seen the man's face too, plainly, in the clear air of the stairwell when they reached the 61st floor. She looked directly at him before he left for the climb back up. That's what she remembered. She thought he might've had a red bandanna, but it wasn't covering his face as they descended the stairs, as he encouraged her to keep going, not to separate from him. She believed he might have had a handkerchief pulled down below his chin, wrapped around his neck, but she wasn't sure. She needed to see his face again to be certain.

Richard showed his mother the attached photo in the message. Ling looked at it, the question hanging in the air.

Both understood how crucial the answer was. To say yes without absolute certainty would be wrong for all involved. They wanted to help Alison, a grieving mother desperate to understand her son's final hour, but they needed to be sure.

Ling couldn't say with certitude. The graduation photo was somehow too formal, the young man in cap and gown too put together, too well groomed. In the escape from the lobby's flames and devastation, the man she remembered reflected the chaos— his short hair matted with sweat, his face flushed. He'd stripped down to his T-shirt. She needed to get a different look at the man to compare with the image trapped in her head.

At Ling's behest, Richard called Alison. He explained he was reaching out, due to his mother's condition, trying to gain more clarity, to confirm whether the man who led Ling down the stairs was in fact Welles. Richard and Ling were determined to confirm Alison's hope, but only if it was true.

"'My mother thinks this may be the man,'" Alison recalled Richard saying. "'But can you send another photograph?'"

Ling wanted a different image, she told her son, "a casual picture of him, something that's not all dressed up, like in a suit and tie."

Alison thought she knew the right shot. "I'll overnight it to you." The picture had to be recent, and clear, out of a suit, Welles in a natural setting. The first image that came to mind was Welles from a year before, standing beside Harry Wanamaker Jr. on the deck of Marine 1's *John D. McKean,* on their cruise around Lower

Manhattan. Behind them, the dark towers of the World Trade Center loomed, soaring into the darkness.

She made a copy of the photo, but altered it first. Alison didn't want the full picture to add in any way to Ling's pain, or influence her decision. She enlarged it from the center until the towers were invisible, cropped from the frame.

Then she sent it to Richard and Ling.

After receiving the second photo, Richard prepared to show it to his mother. He understood the stakes of her reaction, for Ling and for Alison. During their phone conversation, Alison had stressed to Richard that she didn't want to place any pressure on Ling. She was ready to accept a different answer. She could live with *no*.

Richard had his back to Ling, holding the picture, and then turned quickly around. He wanted to see his mother's immediate, raw reaction. Ling looked at the image of Welles's face aboard the boat, the smile broad and easy, the early summer evening, the moment sweet upon the water. Two men, one who would work the pile and come to Alison's door covered with its terrible dirt, and the other, who would be lost somewhere beneath it, inside its crypt, for months. Still lost to her.

Ling looked at the man she'd never seen before September 11, whom she last saw turning around to go back up the stairs to the blood and fire. The face. She looked at nothing more than the face.

One word: Yes.

"I looked at it very carefully," Ling said, recalling the moment.

"My son says, 'Are you sure? Are you one hundred percent sure? You know, you can't be wrong.'"

She didn't hesitate. She was certain.

"If you're going to ask me ten times? Yes. One hundred times? Yes. Because that's the face. . . . That was him, there was no question in my mind."

She didn't know how long it was until the next thought entered her mind, but it would stay there for years to come.

He saved my life.

B efore calling Alison, Ling reached out to Judy first, to share what she saw in the photo, and to build a time line. They could help each other piece together the sequence that led them out of the inferno of the sky lobby, into Stairway A, down to clear air and beyond, to the ground floor, and into the ambulance they shared.

Judy's story shone a light on Ling's own path down the stairwell. Talking with each other, they were struck anew by the improbability of their escape. Ling was the first to answer to Welles's call in the lobby, following him as he led the way into the stairwell, walking with her and the other tall, thin man she didn't know. He walked with them, carrying the woman on his back, until they reached the 61st floor. Then he told her he was going back up. He left to make the ascent back up seventeen floors to 78, to see who else he could help.

When he emerged through the smoke and fire a second time, it was Judy who heard him call out, a man with a red bandanna covering his face against the smoke. She heard his instruction, urgent but strong and clear. They were among the first words she told her husband from her hospital bed hours after the buildings collapsed.

"She heard him call out to everyone," Gerry said. "And he said, 'Everyone who can stand, stand now. If you can help others, do so.' Those were his exact words as she told them to me that afternoon."

At least two others followed Judy into the stairwell, by her account guided there by Welles. Later, after reaching the clear air below the 61st floor, she saw a fire extinguisher. She remembered thinking how strange a place for it, there in the stairwell.

Ling told Judy that this was the fire extinguisher Welles asked her to carry, the one that proved too heavy to lug down. The fire extinguisher helped them understand the sequence—it was Ling who'd gone down first, and then Judy. Welles had helped two different groups of survivors find the stairwell. When Judy reached the 50th floor, she encountered firefighters who were on their way up, exhausted from the climb and the heavy gear they carried. These were the firefighters who told her and the others to continue down to the 40th floor, where they'd find a working service elevator.

More questions remained. How many others had Welles helped? How many of the survivors from the sky lobby followed *them* after Welles's original instruction? They couldn't know.

The call came from Richard.

Before telling Alison, he had a few final questions, to be thorough. To be right. Alison breathed deeply, trying to slow down, to root herself in the moment, not to race ahead.

Alison recounted their conversation vividly. "This red handkerchief that's been mentioned in the article," Richard said to her. "Was it solid red?"

"No," Alison said immediately. "If it was solid red, then that's not Welles. It would have been a bandanna pattern . . ."

"Okay," Richard said. Then another question.

"He was wearing a T-shirt. What kind of T-shirt would it be?"

She knew instantly. He'd worn the same style his whole life, it seemed.

"He would have been wearing a crewneck, short sleeve Brooks Brothers–type white T-shirt." She added, "Not V-neck or tank top."

Richard said that matched his mother's description. How many more questions? She was glad for the tests. She'd told Ling and Judy both, she never wanted to pressure them. She wanted only to know. To fill in the awful blank of the final hour of his life.

No more questions. Just the answer.

"My mother says it's him," Richard told her. "She says this is the man."

Nearly a decade later, in the house on Birchwood, the words still echoed. Reaching back to the moment, Alison fought to describe the meaning. The best accounting came through her tears.

"I finally found him," she said, sobbing. "I finally found him."

Nine and a half months after Judy and Ling shared their cramped, frightened ride in the back of the ambulance, rushing away from the perimeter of the Trade Center complex toward the hospital, they were meeting again in person. Others would join them too—their families and their hosts. On June 23, 2002, they were spending a warm, sunny Sunday afternoon in Upper Nyack, guests of the Crowther family.

Alison had seen Ling and her family already. After their phone conversation, she asked if she could visit with them. She wanted to share so much about Welles, about his life before that moment when he and Ling met. She wanted them to understand her son, as best a mother could explain her child, wondering too if she was being selfish in her need to share him, but Richard's reaction dismissed that concern, according to Alison.

"Richard said to me, 'My mom wanted to know who this man was for a long time.'" The entire family wanted to know.

Alison took some family photo albums, filled with so many of the images that played over and over again in Jeff's slide show, to share the different stages of Welles's life—the boy with his fire truck under the Christmas tree, the one wearing the bandanna across his forehead, the budding lacrosse player, the college kid, the young professional. For Alison, they were portraits of wonder for new eyes to see.

She traveled down to New York Hospital, Cornell Burn Center, where Ling was preparing for her seventh skin graft surgery, to meet Ling, Richard, and their family for lunch. The two women sat beside each other, face-to-face for the first time since Ling made the identification. As painful as Ling's scarring was, as difficult as her recovery continued to be, Alison looked at Ling in awe. She had faced the same fire, breathed the same air, and walked the same steps as her son, and she'd made it down. She said the first thing that came to her mind.

"Thank you so much," Alison said. "I just want to . . ." Her voice trailed away for a few seconds. "I'm so happy to meet you and . . . thank you. Thank you for taking the time to meet with me." She remembered what she carried with her. "I just brought these albums to show you . . . to show you my Welles."

He was almost the sole subject of that first meeting. Ling said virtually nothing about the scene in the sky lobby then, about what she'd endured, about the attacks and the suffering they'd brought her. Alison spoke about Welles, and Ling and her family listened, expressing their gratitude to her as best they could. For raising him. For his help. For his choice.

Now, a few weeks later, they were together again in a larger group—these three families sitting on the shaded patio behind the house on Birchwood, sharing lunch. Ling in a wheelchair with her husband, Don, and their children; Judy with her husband, Gerry; and Alison, Jeff, Honor, Paige, and a few others, all sharing the same table.

At that table, the others listened as Judy and Ling began to talk about the horrors they each endured that day. The descriptions went beyond the time line that led each to understand how Welles had helped them. They spoke about their own suffering, their damaged bodies and haunted visions, the sights never to be unseen. Alison and Jeff were carried into the sky lobby's furnace, and they understood the destruction and death in a way they hadn't before. "They really shared their experiences completely with us," Alison said. The only word she could find to label it was *horror*.

"The horror . . . I just remember thinking how incredibly brave these women are, how they faced what they faced, and have come through it, and are still carrying on. How they were able to re-open all of this so soon to share with us."

Both said Welles had been the only commanding voice they heard, the only one anywhere on the floor who seemed to understand what to do and where to go. With their families around them, each told Alison and Jeff, over and over again, what Welles had done, what he meant to them, what they owed him.

When lunch was over, the tears dried and the plates cleared, they decided there was one more place to go. Judy and Gerry went with Alison, and Ling and her family with Jeff, and the group left the house and headed on a short drive to First Avenue in Nyack. They pulled up outside the stone façade of Grace Episcopal Church. Together, they walked inside, the sanctuary warmer but filled with nearly the same slant of light it held nine months before during the service. The group came to a spot, and turned its gaze upon the church's memorial wall. Jeff and Alison pointed to the place where Welles's ashes lay inside.

The Crowthers were so grateful for the light that had been cast on Welles's final hours. To be able to look into the faces of these two lives he saved, to know their names, to hear their voices. But there were still so many unanswered questions. How many others on the 78th floor might never have seen the red bandanna but had heard a voice, or seen a hand, or followed a lead that came from Welles?

There were tantalizing clues. Two other survivors followed Judy to the stairwell, at least. One of them was Ed Nicholls. He was in the sky lobby waiting for an elevator when the plane's impact blasted him off his feet. He was thrown across the floor, injuring his arm badly when he landed. He had a distinct memory of a man's voice directing him and the others to the stairwell, but not a clear recollection of what he looked like.

Even without more answers, there was a story, and Jeff and Alison wanted to share it—for its message, to help them heal and to help others heal too. They had been granted something so few others had: an understanding of their son's final actions, and their consequences. There was great pride in that knowledge, and no small degree of comfort. They believed the story might prove a point even beyond their son's sacrifice. So many responded by running toward the threat and into the peril. This was the story of one responder, not assigned or asked, not dispatched from a station house or dressed in gear, who did the same and never returned.

Alison believed she knew who would be interested in telling it. Back in March, she'd met Jane Lerner, a veteran reporter with the *Journal News,* a newspaper based in the Lower Hudson Valley and part of the USA TODAY Network across the country. Lerner was assigned to cover the small ceremony at Grace Episcopal after Welles's body was recovered and cremated. Her story, "Volunteer Firefighter Found at Ground Zero Laid to Rest," ran in the Sunday edition of the paper, quoting Alison and rendering the scene with skill and compassion. The piece made an impression on the family.

In June, Alison shared with Lerner the story about her son, the mysterious man noted in the *New York Times* who helped to save others on the 78th floor before losing his life in the South Tower's collapse. Alison told her about Welles, about the red handkerchief he carried since he was a little boy, and, after the planes hit, how he'd swapped his role from equities trader to volunteer firefighter, using the bandanna to cover his face from the smoke and dust as he led others to safety.

The 1,565-word piece ran under the headline BANDANNA LINKS ACTS OF COURAGE, and traced Welles's actions up until, and through, September 11. With quotes from Ling Young and Judy Wein, the story identified Welles Crowther for the first time publicly as the man who saved their lives, and those of an unknown number of others.

"He saved so many people," Young was quoted in the article as saying, "but he didn't save himself."

"His whole life was ahead. It's such a tragedy."

The story was now told.

Soon, it would spread.

The chapel wore its gray proudly, rising like a fortress in native granite. The high-flown arches and opulent carvings looked down upon all who walked its aisles and knelt among its pews. It was a mighty setting for a sacred rite.

Ten months and one day after the towers fell, on July 12, 2002, so many of Welles's childhood and high school friends from Nyack gathered inside as the first among them stood at the altar, awaiting his bride's approach.

Rob Lewis was getting married. He'd known Welles nearly all his life in Nyack, all the way back to playing T-ball games together and being in the same Cub Scout troop, where Alison served as den mother. As each grew, their bond hardened over afternoons of pond hockey and through the seasons of their lacrosse careers. Of all the friends who gave Welles grief while growing up, Lewis was likely the toughest. He would be the first to admit it. But friends they remained, delivering and receiving each other's jabs while protecting each other from anyone else's. After graduation they moved in separate directions, Lewis continuing his lacrosse career just twenty-seven miles north up the Hudson Valley, at West Point.

While Welles walked the paths of Chestnut Hill with his lax stick over his shoulder and Lewis endured plebe life and formation drills and combat training, they stayed in touch, part of the larger Nyack crew who saw one another during holidays and summers and reunions back home.

Lewis's fiancée, Liz Chambers, whom he had dated since high school, was a lacrosse standout for Nyack as well. After graduating, she played at Rutgers. Lewis remembered one visit he and Welles made to see her. The two stayed in Liz's apartment for the weekend, and during a party there, a fracas broke out. Lewis looked over to see Welles in the center of a fight, slamming another partygoer to the floor and rolling around with him.

"He was never a bully," Lewis said of Welles, "but he was tough. There were a bunch of drunk college guys, and he saw one going into her room. He didn't like it."

After graduating, Lewis proposed to Liz while stationed at Fort Stewart in Georgia before leaving for a posting in Kosovo as an army officer. They knew it would be a large wedding. Liz had five siblings and a long roster of friends and teammates. The side of the altar would be crowded. That was perfect for Lewis. He wanted as many of his friends there to stand beside him as would come. Ultimately, it was decided. Liz would have eight bridesmaids; Lewis, nine groomsmen. Welles was among the first he asked.

When the planes struck the towers, Lewis was forty-six hundred miles east, in Kosovo. He remembered a group of fifty soldiers packed into a room in their camp, watching the smoke and fire unfurl across the television screen. He'd never felt so maddeningly far from his country. Soon after, he was attached to an e-mail chain, including Welles's address, connecting Nyack friends, searching for any information. As days, and then weeks, passed, the dispatches grew less frequent, until the communications stopped completely. All understood the silence.

Just a few weeks before the wedding, the story of Welles's final hour began to make the rounds, from one friend to another, one e-mail and call to the next, in a spreading pool of recognition. What he'd done. Who he'd saved. The story was at once astonishing and real. The friends and their families had to share it with one another, and with others outside the circle too, with people who never knew Welles.

By the time Rob Lewis and Liz Chambers kissed each other for the first time as husband and wife, walking down the aisle past Jeff and Alison and more than a hundred others there to celebrate them, stepping out into their first moments of a new life, they'd already made room for one guest who wasn't there. When the bride and groom were introduced at the reception, the wedding party lining up to greet them, Lewis walked in beaming, an enormous smile on his face, his arms raised high. In his hand, he held a red bandanna. All the groomsmen, including his brother, Steven, and his army buddy Jimmy Silliman, and all the Nyack gang— Karim Raoul, Jody Steinglass, Willie Hopkins, Matt Dickey, Michael Barch, Matt Drowne—had red bandannas in their jacket pockets. They lifted them high.

They were carrying Welles to the party.

And so it started. From an e-mail Alison sent to those who'd reached out in the first days and weeks after the attacks to the friends desperate to know if he'd made it out, she decided to share the story—not focused on Welles's death or the way he'd died. Everyone knew that already. This message was about what he'd done just before his death, the details of where and how he'd done it, and for whom. She didn't dwell on the reasons. All receiving the note knew Welles, so they already understood.

The story pushed past the friends, beyond Boston and Nyack and Rockland County, down the Lower Hudson Valley into New York City, and from there, across the country. CNN. *USA TODAY.* ABC News. There was a flurry of coverage in particular as the first anniversary arrived, spotlighting the tale of a young man who climbed back up as others went down. But after the anniversary passed, as powerful as the story was, Jeff and Alison could feel the momentum gently slow, and the spread stall.

They didn't stop, though. Together with the help of friends and a close board of advisers, they created a charitable trust in Welles's name, determined to find and build good from his death, to share the meaning of his life and his sacrifice. It was essential to their own survival to find some light. Their goal was not just to remember but, through memory, to give. Starting the year after his death, the trust began granting scholarships to Nyack students who embodied Welles's values and passions, and making gifts and grants to other nonprofits sharing his example. The trust required a great deal of work in its creation, but the work provided its own measure of healing.

As for its symbol, in time that would spread in ways no trust could ever seed.

The hollow in the ground remained. Fights over the site's future persisted. But some of the wounds to the city's psyche, and to the country's, started to close, if not in healing or acceptance, then through the unremitting push of time. The pulse of the tragedy grew fainter if it didn't course through you each day— marked by the empty chair, or the silent phone, or the vacant room at home.

For those Welles left, there was a simple fabric in the absence, a red piece of him that resisted any fading. Somehow, the bandanna mattered, its knot tying together his memory and example to those who still held them, and might perpetuate them.

His friends began carrying his story inside the handkerchief's folds.

John Scott, his teammate in Nyack, ran a youth hockey program in Raleigh, North Carolina, and told every player about the bandanna and the man behind it. The same was true for the women's college softball team Scott helped at his alma mater, Barton College, in Wilson, North Carolina. "For every team I coach, nobody wears number nineteen," he said, "and I tell the kids why."

Tyler Jewell, his friend and teammate at BC, represented the United States as a snowboarder in the Winter Olympics in Turin in 2006, competing in the men's parallel giant slalom. Though he didn't win gold, Jewell wore his own medal to the games, one made of cloth. He wrapped the red bandanna around his neck for the world to see as he slashed down the mountain.

Matt O'Keefe, a college classmate and avid golfer, tied a bandanna around the handle of his golf bag the week Welles's body was recovered, and never removed it. After BC, he founded an apparel company for CrossFit athletes, several of whom would wear the bandanna design O'Keefe created. "They have such an attachment to that story," O'Keefe said. "It's become a symbol of strength and courage."

Chris Varmon, another hockey teammate in Nyack, helped to create the Red Bandanna Skate for young and old players of all skills in Rockland County, an event to celebrate sportsmanship, team spirit, and passion for the game. Each year, most of the skaters wear bandannas beneath their helmets, as Welles often did.

Matt Drowne, another friend from Nyack, went a step further. He had a tattoo of the bandanna inked between his shoulders, with Welles's initials placed at the bottom. As a teacher and administrator working with special needs students, he began a red bandanna award, given each year to a child demonstrating exceptional courage.

Jessica Alberti, a friend from BC, remembered Welles as a kind voice during the challenges of their college years. After learning what Welles had done, she pushed herself to run her first marathon. In 2002, she crossed the line in Central Park after 26.2 miles through New York City, with Welles's name written across her shirt and a small red bandanna attached. "I felt like if he could do something that amazing," Alberti said, "I should be able to do this." In 2004, she and others helped to start the annual Red Bandanna 5k at Boston College, now one of the biggest events on campus each fall.

Tim Epstein, a friend who lived in the same freshman dorm at BC, would present Welles's story to the board of the Fetzer Institute, a foundation with a deep endowment working to promote love and forgiveness around the world. Through the presentation, Fetzer would help to fund a character-based curriculum (developed by Alison, Jeff, and others) for schools around the country to teach lessons of service and compassion through Welles's story and the bandanna's symbol. When Epstein's wife gave birth to their daughter, he called Jeff and Alison from the hospital to ask a favor. "I wanted to make sure that they would be comfortable with us naming her Madeline Welles," he said. "They gave the blessing, and we announced her to the world thereafter." Other such announcements would come as children were named after Welles in numbers unseen before. Before 2012, there were no more than five children in the United States who were given the name Welles in a single year. Between 2012 and 2014, there were thirty-five newborns given the name—many in families who'd never met Welles or the Crowthers.

Chris Reynolds knew Welles from childhood but understood the symbol of the bandanna differently from anyone else. A friend growing up, a teammate in football and hockey, he remembered joking in a high school locker room that he and the other guys "would be flipping burgers, and Welles will be making a difference in the world someday." The others laughed, Welles maybe the loudest. But Reynolds would make his own considerable mark. He too became a volunteer firefighter as a teenager, and knew immediately it would be his career. After attending college, getting the FDNY application, taking the exams, staying in shape, waiting, the call came. His first posting was with New York City EMS, which had just come under the FDNY's control. A short time later, in February 2001, he made the move to "probie school," the department's probationary firefighter program. After ten weeks he graduated, and in the spring he received his first appointment. Engine 80, Harlem. A lifelong dream achieved, was how he described it.

The morning of September 11, Reynolds was at work when a second alarm transmitted, indicating a plane had struck the World Trade Center. He and others turned to the house television.

"We see the smoke coming out of the building," Reynolds remembered, "and everything that's happening downtown, and we start getting ready. We're going to get a response to head down to the Trade Center. We did a refill on all of the medical equipment and getting ready to go, waiting for the dispatcher to send us downtown.

"And then we saw the second plane hit."

As one of the last units left in Upper Manhattan, Reynolds's company endured an agonizing wait before being dispatched to the scene, not arriving until after dark. The site was overwhelming in its destruction, the twisted shards of steel reaching upward from the pile like bones through skin. He arrived with his company Tuesday night, and didn't leave for five days.

"We still thought it was going to be a rescue operation," he said. "We would get some people out alive. There were a lot of names going around, people who were missing. . . . There were a lot of firemen's names." Hundreds were unaccounted for, some Reynolds knew, all who shared his calling, his brotherhood.

Thursday, he saw Harry Wanamaker on the pile. They hugged each other in their relief, grateful each was alive. Wanamaker told him that Welles was among the missing. As days turned to a week, it became clear to them both that there were no more lives to save, only remains to recover. Like Wanamaker, Reynolds worked the pile, returning to the site week after week for months. Wanamaker would die of cancer in 2010, his family believing his death was caused by the time he spent inhaling the toxic fumes at the site. Few could understand what the recovery workers endured, or their dedication.

"Going down there," Reynolds said, "was almost therapeutic. I didn't want *not* to be on the pile. Every time we got released, to be at home or go sleep, all you were doing was going to funerals. I'd rather be working, at least helping families with some closure, than not be there." He wasn't there when Welles's body was found, but knew the area well, and understood where Welles was, and why.

"I know he was found with Ladder 4 in the lobby," he said. "I'm sure he was standing right there with his brothers, waiting to go back up and help. . . . I'm sure he was helping the chief, the command post, and the officers of the companies and the firemen, to let them know what the best route was, because he came down from the upper floors. He obviously had a path, he'd let them know what stairwell he used, and I'm sure he gave them a sense of what was going on in the upper floors. I mean, he just went through hell."

Reynolds paused.

"He had every opportunity to leave and he didn't. He stayed and he put others first and that's something you either have or you don't. He had it, and he used it."

Even after the funerals were finished, and the pile cleared, and the anniversaries commemorated, as the years passed, Reynolds never allowed the memory to fade. Above the banister outside his house, there is a red bandanna tied to one of the rails, and he passes it every day as he leaves for his next shift.

"I have two little girls," Reynolds said more than a decade after the towers fell.

"A four-year-old and a two-year-old. My girls ask about the bandanna, 'What's that for?' I tell them, 'It's for Daddy's friend, a friend that did a lot of good for a lot of people. Daddy's friend is up in heaven,' and I don't say any more."

On a December day, with temperatures in the fifties, Jeff and Alison led a small caravan traveling south to the city for a ceremony they never thought they'd witness. They gathered at MetroTech Plaza in downtown Brooklyn, off Flatbush Avenue, ten days before Christmas for an event held just once before in the 141 years since the department's founding. It was only the second time the FDNY would posthumously name someone an honorary member of its ranks.

The idea had its seed in a chance encounter. Lee Ielpi, who joined the FDNY in 1970, had lost his son Jonathan in the attacks when he responded as a member of FDNY Squad 288. Ielpi had spent months on the recovery effort at ground zero, and he was on the pile when Assistant Chief Donald Burns was found in late March 2002 in the ruins of the South Tower's lobby, along with the remains of several other firefighters, and Welles's own.

Months after his son was recovered, Jeff went downtown to the Family Room, on Liberty Plaza, a space adjacent to ground zero where victims' loved ones could come for privacy and reflection. One of the rooms was solely for immediate family, its walls covered with photos and mementos. Jeff brought a photo in a simple wooden frame to add to the collection. While there, Jeff encountered Ielpi, and the two began to talk. Ielpi explained that he too had lost his son in the attacks, among the 343 FDNY members who were killed. Jeff told him that Welles was a volunteer firefighter, and that his remains were found on March 19 in the lobby's rubble.

"You have to remember where the lobby was when we got to it," Ielpi would later recall about the pile's slow, brutal clearing. "It was below grade. It collapsed down with all the weight of the floors above it. We were quite a ways down. Jeff said the reports were that Welles was right in that area, with Donald Burns. So I had to think about it for a second and I figured, 'Let me tell him, let me tell him.'"

After months of the solemn but tedious work flanking the heavy machinery, watching the mechanical jaws sift through the mangled steel and pulverized concrete, and always searching for any hint or flash of something in the rubble, something fragile and human, flesh or bone, the days blended together. But not those few days in March, not the day Burns was found. That day Ielpi remembered clearly. And meeting Jeff, the memory came back.

"I was underneath a very large beam and there were some remains there," Ielpi later recalled. "When Jeff said that about Chief

Burns, who I knew very well, I said to him, 'Jeff, I want you to know that I found Donald Burns.' And he started crying and he said, 'Well, you found my son.' I said, 'I cannot say I found your son, that's not fair. I cannot say that. I can tell you I was there with Donald Burns, and there were quite a large number of human remains in that area. Maybe one of them was your son, I would hope so. He still gave me a big hug and said, 'You found my son.'

"We left it in that general idea, that I was there when Welles's remains were found."

Ielpi never forgot the conversation, nor the story of the man in the red bandanna, and a few years later, he played a role in helping this day take its shape. Upstairs at the FDNY headquarters in Brooklyn, in a plain room with beige walls, the Crowthers gathered alongside department officials, including Fire Commissioner Nicholas Scoppetta and Chief of Department Salvatore Cassano, the leaders of the FDNY. The ceremony was short and to the point, and so were the remarks.

"This is the least we could do," said Scoppetta. "He had everything to live for, and his parents can take comfort in the fact—if it's possible to take comfort under these circumstances—that he died while helping others."

Standing on the right side of the podium, facing the local news cameras and a small group of reporters, Jeff tried to stay composed.

"We are honoring a true hero," Cassano said. "He had the genes of a New York City firefighter."

The commissioner and chief of the department named Welles a member, forever a part of its rolls, a brother among the bravest. At the end of the ceremony, Alison and Jeff were presented with a framed special commendation, a certificate of appointment for Welles, acknowledging his place in the ranks along with the more than eleven thousand others under the department's command. The frame was heavy and solid in their hands. It was proof that their son was recognized in a way he'd dreamed about since he was a boy.

Four years before, two months after the attacks, Jeff had held another piece of paper, unframed and less formal. On a cold November day, Jeff and Alison had gone to the apartment on Washington Place, to clean out Welles's belongings and take them home. The trip was necessary but almost unbearable. The evidence of his interrupted life was crushing in its detail, in the mute simplicity of his possessions: the suits still hanging in the closet, the empty shoes waiting beneath them, the photos of family on the bedside table, the sweatpants in the drawers.

Going through Welles's papers, Jeff found the tangible manifestation of Welles's wish to change his life. It was a city form. Standing in the apartment, Jeff looked down at the small type and understood the depth of his son's dream. Welles had gone past imagining or talk. He'd begun. There, in the apartment, Jeff looked down at the paper, an application to the FDNY, several of the lines already filled in, dated just a month before his death.

Now, four years later, Jeff hoped Welles would know—that although some of the lines would forever be blank, his application was received, his submission reviewed.

Yes, Welles. You were accepted.

Alison had nodded off on a couch near the back of the house, the television throwing colors across the room, its chatter blending into the rhythms of her breathing. Spring had arrived, and the yard was stirring to life. It was late on a Sunday night, not quite eleven P.M., she thought. A crime procedural had been on as she'd drifted off, and now, coming to, she dimly perceived that the case had been cracked. She heard the authoritative voices speaking, part of the formula.

Then she saw the image. The white turban. The flowing black beard specked with gray below the chin. The Kalashnikov rifle slung over the shoulder. The most wanted man on the face of the earth. She saw his face, and below it, she read the words: *"Osama bin Laden, killed."*

Startled, she stood up, confused and then outraged. How could a television drama use the death of a man who claimed responsibility for 9/11 as some plotline prop, as entertainment? Who would do this? It was offensive, and wrong. It was too soon.

Then she looked closer, her mind clearing and her heart racing. The show was apparently interrupted, or over. It was not a series. It was a news set, or images of the White House exterior, and again, the pictures of bin Laden. The news anchors were sharing what they knew, obvious excitement pushing against their attempts to be measured. The words scrolled across the bottom of the screen. Could this be real? She heard anchors promise a presidential address.

Standing up in the room alone, she felt her chest constrict tightly. And then the coil inside her let go, and she burst into tears. She ran toward the stairs.

"All this emotion," Alison said, "bottled up inside of me . . ."

All of it came out in wails and tears, the black block of ice inside her that would never melt, hardened by frustration and rage, despair and fury, freezing some part of her insides for ten solid years, and now it cracked and splintered. The hollow refrain that ran through her—*Why can't they get this guy? Why can't they get him?!!*—stopped.

"Jeff!" she yelled down the stairs. "Jeff! They got him! They got him!"

Jeff was already watching, trying to process the news. He came up and saw Alison in tears. "Why are you crying?" he asked, embracing her. "This is great news."

A short time later, at 11:35 P.M., the president stepped to a lectern in the White House to tell the nation and the world that Osama bin Laden was dead. After announcing the operation that killed the Al Qaeda leader, he harkened back to the terrorist attacks at the World Trade Center and the Pentagon, and the wreckage of United Flight 93 in Shanksville, Pennsylvania. Less than a minute into his remarks, his message grew more personal, his tone softer. He looked directly into the network pool camera, and spoke as if directly to the two people standing in a house in Upper Nyack.

"The worst images are those that were unseen to the world," the president said. "The empty seat at the dinner table. Children who were forced to grow up without their mother or their father. Parents who would never know the feeling of their child's embrace."

They both listened, maybe even nodding, burdened with an understanding of such terrible truth.

At some point, the date occurred to them. May 1, 2011. It was Jeff and Alison's fortieth wedding anniversary. Later, when they spoke to Paige and Honor, the sisters would immediately credit their brother.

"That was a gift from Welles," they said.

. . .

The next morning, Alison was at the computer checking e-mail, still processing the news overnight, when she received a message with an official-looking insignia attached. The note indicated that the president was preparing to visit ground zero, and if she would like to attend a private event to meet him, she needed to provide pertinent information for a necessary background check. The message asked for her Social Security number and other personal material.

Scam, she thought. No way would she provide the information to a confusing, unknown sender with a government address, buried in an avalanche of letters and slashes. Her finger hovered over the delete key but then retreated. Her head was still buzzing with the president's speech and the notion of bin Laden gone. She clicked open the form and provided the information. She hit SEND and closed the screen.

Three days later, on a sunny windswept Thursday, Alison and Jeff traveled to Lower Manhattan. This was President Obama's first visit to the site since taking office. On previous anniversaries of the attacks, in 2009 and 2010, he'd paid his respects at the memorial at the Pentagon. This day, he came instead to the site where the overwhelming majority of lives were lost and to its deepest scar, to pay tribute to the victims of the attacks and to meet with their families as well as with firefighters, police officers, and other first responders. It was not a day for speeches. His presence was meant both as symbol and as salve—to honor those lost, and to represent justice done.

Before arriving at the site, the president stopped to spend time at

Engine 54 on West Forty-eighth Street in Manhattan. Inside the firehouse, he ate lunch with firefighters and looked at photos on the walls, a patchwork of lives lost, portraits of an entire shift of men who rushed to the towers after the first plane hit, all now dead.

Later, at the site where the Twin Towers once stood, with construction halted and large cranes looming above him, the president laid a wreath at the base of a tree recovered from amid the ruins, replanted, and somehow restored to full leaf. Afterward, he retreated to an area out of public view, without press. He visited the preview site for the 9/11 Memorial Museum, set up across the street from St. Paul's Chapel on lower Broadway, the church that miraculously survived the terrorist attacks a block away without a single window broken. The chapel had served as refuge for those working at the site for months afterward, and stood to many as an emblem of God's grace.

In the preview center's simple setting, Jeff, Alison, and roughly sixty other family members of victims waited at tables of eight set up for the president's visit. All guests were checked and vetted, having passed facial recognition tests. Several early exhibits had already been designed and set up, awaiting transfer to the museum's permanent home, its opening still a few years away. One of the exhibits was dedicated to Welles. Jeff and Alison drifted to it as if to stand near him.

Just then, the door swung open and the president entered. Alison was immediately struck by Barack Obama's presence, less formal, more radiant, different from the hundreds of times she'd seen him as an image on television, or pressed into a newspaper photo. She and Jeff had both been briefed about the visit. The president wanted to spend time with the families privately. Beyond that, they didn't know how much time he would spend, if they would speak to him directly. They had little real sense of what to expect from the visit. Her first glimpse surprised her. Here he was, on the other side of the room, so close, moving so easily from family to family, person to person, speaking with each one.

In the next moment, the president approached them, extending his hand, looking directly into their faces. Alison was clutching a red bandanna, squeezing it tightly in her hand, a piece not just of her son's life but of hers. Jeff put out his hand and said, "Mr. President, I'm the father of Welles Remy–" The president cut him off: "Crowther," he said.

"I know about your son," the president continued. "The man with the red bandanna." Whether he'd learned just that morning or long before was meaningless to them. The acknowledgment was astounding. The president knew their son's name, knew his story. It was unfathomable, yet as clear as the man standing before them.

"Thank you," Alison said, the first words that rushed out of her, looking at him. It wasn't gratitude for the acknowledgment. This came from a more primal, visceral place. "Thank you for getting the job done." She didn't feel she was speaking to a nation's leader right then, to the commander in chief who had ordered the mission.

"It was a feeling of one parent talking with another," she remembered years later. "Commiserating." As much as his praise for Welles's courage that day touched them, the president also spoke to them about their loss, and their coping. He told them he couldn't imagine losing one of his children, and marveled at the strength they possessed in enduring it.

As the president was about to leave, Alison didn't hesitate. She had to ask him a favor.

"Would you be willing to take a photo with us, Mr. President, near Welles's exhibit?" she asked. He agreed, telling them to stand by the display and wait for him there after he'd met with all the families in the room. They moved to the part of the room where Welles was memorialized and stood near his picture, wondering if Barack Obama would stop back. He did.

He put his arms around Jeff and Alison and posed for a picture. And before leaving, Alison asked for one moment more. Would he be willing to sign a red bandanna for her? She had two ready.

The president reached for his pen, bent over, and signed the red fabric. Above his name, he inscribed a simple message.

"We won't forget Welles."

Exactly when it changed from a story to a mission, he couldn't say. But he knew he was called to tell it to the country.

Drew Gallagher and Welles first met as wide-eyed freshmen, each worried about little more than catching the bus to the main campus, keeping their class schedules straight, and acclimating to the pressurized freedoms of life away from home. Over the next four years, they crossed paths often, in the same parties and the same bars. They played intramural hockey games together and hung out in larger groups afterward. Their friends were friends, and the different crowds often melded together.

After graduating, when Welles went to Wall Street, Gallagher entered a field many of his buddies dreamed about but few ultimately pursued: sports. After spending the summer as an intern for the BankBoston Classic, an event on the Senior PGA Tour, he landed a job at NESN, the New England Sports Network, one of the most successful regional sports broadcasters in the country. He worked there as a special projects coordinator for just three months before getting the call he most wanted. In February 2000, he joined ESPN as a production assistant.

Gallagher was more than a sports junkie or someone with encyclopedic recall and knowledge of stats and jersey numbers and arcane records. A good athlete himself as a hockey and a baseball player, he wanted to get off the corporate campus in Bristol, Connecticut, and out in the field whenever he could, to interview players and coaches, to shine a light on the backstories beyond their exploits. Cutting highlights was a start, but he wanted to tell stories. A creative thinker, he discovered that the fastest way to a role in feature producing was to pitch ideas in volume. The more pitches, the better the chances to be assigned to produce and tell the story, from arranging and conducting interviews to crafting scripts to overseeing the edits that shaped the material into televised life. He climbed quickly, producing stories for NHL and NFL shows at first, before earning a spot as a full-fledged feature producer in 2006.

The last time he'd seen Welles was on an escalator in Grand Central Terminal in the summer of 2001. They were moving in opposite directions, Gallagher headed up from the subway platforms and Welles headed down. They shouted their greetings to each other, the conversation swept away by the moving stairs. The encounter lasted less than fifteen seconds.

Gallagher first pitched the idea to his bosses for the five-year anniversary of 9/11, as a story about a former athlete who died in the attacks after saving the lives of others caught in the South Tower. He didn't think the story needed an overwhelming sports hook; the nature of Welles's sacrifice was compelling enough on its own. But his lacrosse career mattered, and would present him as an athlete to an audience of sports fans.

The bosses passed. Whether it was fatigue from all the stories the network had already done about the day, the feeling that the sports hook wasn't pronounced enough, or the fact that another feature about 9/11 was already in production, Gallagher understood the rejection. He pitched ideas all the time, and only a handful were green-lighted. He understood, but he didn't accept.

Over the next several years, he continued to pitch Welles's story. As a Boston College alum, he'd seen the Red Bandanna Run on campus grow steadily, and believed a longer feature on Welles's life would move people who'd never met him, simply through the valor and sacrifice of what he'd done. With the approach of the tenth anniversary, he pitched the story again. This time, the bosses gave the go-ahead.

Gallagher had already done a lot of preproduction work, reaching out to Alison and Jeff, gathering footage, lining up other interview subjects, when he asked if I'd be interested in joining the project. I served as the reporter and writer for the feature, which was narrated by native New Yorker, actor, and director Ed Burns.

The piece ran thirteen and a half minutes, debuting the first week of September 2011. The reaction came quickly.

"His story had come out," Alison said. "In the initial year there was media coverage, and every September 11 there was some talk of it. But once the ESPN story hit . . . wow. It launched . . ."

"Welles's story was out there," Paige said, "but the piece was the tipping point."

In the days following, the reaction grew and spread, nearly overwhelming the family. Teachers showed the piece to their students, coaches to their teams, parents to their children, and children to their parents, many of them writing letters to Jeff and Alison. A team in New Zealand competing in the Rugby World Cup wore red bandannas as a way to honor Welles. A news crew from France interviewed Jeff and Alison about the meaning of the symbol. And less than a week later, two students from the University of Central Florida started a social media campaign, asking their classmates to wear the red handkerchiefs when their football team, the Knights, hosted Boston College on September 10. BC's athletic department caught wind of the students' push. Paige, and Honor, who went on to write a children's book about her brother, both made the trip to Orlando to represent the family.

Even before they walked into Bright House Stadium Welles's two sisters, both of whom also graduated from BC, saw the bandannas everywhere, outside in the tailgating lots, worn by fans as they walked through the turnstiles. When they reached the field, they were stunned as they looked into the stands. Nearly the entire student section, more than five thousand strong, was paying tribute to their brother, waving bandannas for a man they'd never met, an alumnus of the opposing school. It wouldn't be the last time a surge of red would flash through a stadium in homage to Welles.

In the years to come, the piece would air every year on September 11. Posted on the Internet by dozens of sites, the video drew millions of views. Maybe some already knew the story, while others heard Welles's name for the first time. Maybe some were sports fans, while others were simply proud of one man's courage in the final measure of his life. Maybe there were some moved by Jeff's emotion, or Alison's strength, or Welles's valor.

Maybe the story caught the eye of one viewer who already knew some of its details. This viewer had a passion for sports, playing pickup basketball and the occasional round of golf, watching games and highlights and checking the scores and standings when his schedule allowed, if only to escape from the weight and stress of his day. Maybe there was something in the story that reminded him of the mother and father he'd met a few months earlier, of a bandanna she presented and he autographed, and a message he wrote above his name.

We won't forget Welles.

Two and a half years later, he proved the message right.

The president of the United States remembered the red bandanna.

S he'd never returned.

For more than thirteen years, through countless days in hospitals and dozens of surgeries, across punishing hours of therapy and the never-ending pain of the rehab sessions, amid all the nightmarish visions and the annual recitation of the names, in the ceremonies and anniversaries and milestones, she never came back. Even when she looked at his picture, frozen and ageless against time, sitting on a table next to the sofa in her living room in New Jersey, she didn't allow her mind to travel back. She focused only on the face and the name. Not the day. Not the place.

Ling Young knew how difficult it would be to step back inside, to walk into the hollow where the towers once stood, across the ground where she once worked and so many friends and colleagues perished. If she viewed coming back as a descent into a tomb from which she escaped, if there was some healing to find or reckoning to face in walking once more in the space where the World Trade Center once soared, she didn't say. She came on this day not by her choice, but because of a friend's request.

Alison asked her to come.

May 14, 2014, marked the long-awaited opening of the National September 11 Memorial Museum in New York City. The discussions and disputes over its creation formed soon after the ruins were cleared, lasting through years of delay and acrimony. The victims' families, though bound by loss, would never reach a consensus on the way to honor their loved ones best. Some found the museum's location offensive and insensitive, a gallery atop the still unrecovered remains of their lost. Others saw it as disrespectful to share a space beside a private repository where unidentified remains were stored. The museum and plaza above had cost more than half a billion dollars to construct.

But others believed in its mission, contributed to its displays and collections, and found a quiet and deep honor in having their kin remembered and their lives commemorated in a place of permanence for generations to see. Its public unveiling would come in a week. This day was for a carefully selected crowd, seven hundred invited guests gathering far belowground, inside the museum's soaring central hall. The ceremony was set for broadcast around the country.

The Crowthers were not only on the guest list. Alison would be called onstage, the first speaker to follow the president. He'd be introducing her, and Ling Young as well, the two women scheduled to walk to the stage together once the president finished his remarks. The White House reached out to Alison a week earlier and, over a series of calls, gently broached the idea of having her give a brief speech of her own. By the third call, she realized she was being vetted by the staff, to be certain she was willing and capable. Barack Obama's director of speechwriting, Terry Szuplat, spent nearly an hour on the phone with her, reviewing Welles's life, mining her memories, to prepare for the president's remarks. Initially, Alison was told she'd have forty-five seconds of her own to speak. The time seemed to her impossibly short, and immensely important.

The night before, the Crowthers and Youngs had dinner together, as they had many times over the years since their first meeting in 2002, at the hospital burn center. They stayed in a hotel in Lower Manhattan, but not in the financial district. Ling liked the location, especially for its distance from the site. She didn't want to be any closer to ground zero than necessary before the ceremony.

The families arrived together early the next day, along with Honor, her husband, Rick, and their four children, and Paige and her fiancé, Jarrod. Their seats were in the second row, and walking to them they saw the names reserved for the chairs directly in front of theirs. Their seats were behind Bill and Hillary Clinton.

Jeff and Alison were in the same row, but across an aisle. Before the ceremony began, Alison and Ling were led from their seats to a place backstage behind a large screen set up for images to be displayed during the event. There was a monitor placed there, for them to watch what unfolded on the other side of the screen.

But it was the sound at the ceremony's start that reached inside Alison, stopping her. A children's choir onstage and in an upper balcony began the program with a rendition of "Somewhere," from *West Side Story,* the play's most yearning anthem.

"When I heard the children sing," she said, "I started coming apart." She listened, trying to breathe deeply, to clear her mind, to focus on the short speech she'd written with Jeff, playing it through her memory. She was also deeply aware of Ling's nerves and apprehension, not only at being back here but at playing a role, coping with the weight of attention placed on her. Speaking in her second language, Ling was going to introduce Alison, her face and voice projected on the screen. They sat together, waiting to be called. They listened as an honor guard made its march down the center aisle, toward the stage, turning to face the assembly as the choir then sang the national anthem.

Michael Bloomberg, the former mayor of New York City, was the first to speak, and after brief remarks, he introduced Barack Obama to the stage. On the run of the program, the president was given three minutes—an extraordinarily short time, given the moment's import and solemnity. Alison sensed he would speak longer than that, and knew her son would be included somewhere in the body of his remarks; to what extent, she had little idea.

Obama took long strides up the steps and moved behind the presidential lectern. He addressed the mayor, the governor, the guests, and the families of the fallen. Immediately after, he began to describe the scene on the 78th floor of the South Tower, mentioning the fire, the smoke, the darkness, the despair in the sky lobby's sudden wreckage. He paused, allowing the image to linger across the room.

"And then there came a voice," the president said. "Clear, calm, saying he had found the stairs. A young man in his twenties, strong, emerged from the smoke, and over his nose and his mouth he wore a red handkerchief."

Alison, behind the screen, felt the breath inside her seize. The president continued.

"He called for fire extinguishers to fight back the flames. He tended to the wounded. He led those survivors down the stairs to safety, and carried a woman on his shoulders down seventeen flights. Then he went back. Back up all those flights . . . bringing more wounded to safety. Until that moment when the tower fell.

"They didn't know his name. They didn't know where he came from. But they knew their lives had been saved by the man in the red bandanna."

The president spoke of the loss of nearly three thousand souls, saying the museum would forever provide a place "to touch their names, and hear their voices and glimpse the small items that speak to the beauty of their lives."

But he singled out one life, and uttered one name, and described one man to the room, to the world.

"Welles was just twenty-four years old, with a broad smile and a bright future," the president said, as images of Welles flashed across the large screen behind him, the colors spilling into the space where Alison and Ling sat, waiting.

"He had a big laugh, a joy of life, and dreams of seeing the world. He worked in finance, but he had also been a volunteer firefighter. And after the planes hit, he put on that bandanna and spent his final moments saving others."

The speech lasted nine minutes, and at its conclusion, Obama called for the two guests waiting backstage to come forward.

"It is my honor to introduce two women forever bound by that day," the president said, "united in their determination to keep alive the true spirit of 9/11—Welles Crowther's mother, Alison, and one of those he saved, Ling Young."

As they emerged into view, holding hands as they climbed the tall steps toward the podium, the president turned toward them and began to clap, along with the rest of the audience. He greeted them, kissing Ling on the cheek, and then bending forward with a full reach to embrace Alison, her arms wrapping around him. Walking toward their separate lectern, Alison tried to remain composed, to keep her mind clear, with one goal, when she spoke.

"I wanted to show strength, not weakness," she said.

Ling began. "I'm here today because of Welles," she said, her voice strong and clear. "It was very hard for me to come here today, but I wanted to do so, so I could say thank you to his parents and my new friends, Jeff and Alison."

Alison looked at Ling, thanked her, and exhaled as she turned to the microphone. She spoke of her son in the present tense, not the past.

"My husband, Jefferson, and I could not be more proud of our son," she said. "For us, he lives on in the people he helped and in the memory of what he chose to do that Tuesday in September. Welles believes that we are all connected as one human family, that we are here to look out for and to care for one another."

From his seat in the second row, Jeff looked up at Alison and mouthed the words as his wife spoke them. Each had committed the speech to memory. As Alison continued, Jeff recited the lines silently, with tears in his eyes.

"It is our greatest hope," she said, her voice ringing through the hall, "that when people come here and see Welles's red bandanna, they will remember how people helped each other that day. And we hope that they will be inspired to do the same, in ways both big and small. This is the true legacy of September 11."

Her voice carried north to Midtown, into the offices of Sandler O'Neill, sixty-six of whose employees came to work on the 104th floor that September day and never returned. Thirteen years later, survivors like Mark Fitzgibbon, Karen Fishman, and John Kline would hear her, as would the firm's leader, Jimmy Dunne. In the years since the attacks, Dunne had rebuilt the company from the ashes of its mourning, more than doubling its ranks and strengthening its place on Wall Street. The firm had done more than endure. It prevailed, and was thriving. Dunne looked upon Welles with immense pride.

Her words reached west to Ohio, where Natalie McIver could hear them. In the days that followed 9/11, after she saw the first plane hit the tower from the deck of a Hudson ferry, after she slept in rather than coming in early, she worked in Sandler's call center, reaching out to the families. The calls were crushing with the tonnage of grief, and she fought against the weight, trying to help. She went to Welles's memorial at Grace Episcopal, among the dozens of other services, before eventually leaving New York City. But she kept a journal in the days after the attacks, and in it, Welles and other colleagues' memories endured.

Alison's speech echoed through the sunken ground where John Ryan, commander of the Port Authority Police Department's rescue and recovery operation at ground zero, who'd spent months at work on the pile, might hear about one man's sacrifice among so many. Like others familiar with the dimensions of the lobby and the location of its command center, he knew how close Welles was to making it out. As the former acting chief of the department, and a detective lieutenant of its joint terrorism task force, he worked to make sure no one would face such a sacrifice in the city again.

Alison's remarks lasted exactly sixty seconds. When she was done, she paused for the slightest moment, looking out into the gathering. She looked down, and exhaled. With Ling by her side, she turned and left the stage.

It was September 13, 2014, a Saturday night in Chestnut Hill, and the Boston College Eagles football team was already down 17–6 before the end of the first quarter. They were facing another beating at the hands of a perennial college football powerhouse.

The game against USC was just following script as an obvious mismatch. The Trojans were ranked ninth in the country, a preseason pick by many to win the Pac-12 conference and a strong candidate for the first ever college football playoff at season's end. Pundits from ESPN to *Sports Illustrated* had tabbed the Trojans as a national championship contender. Already notching a big win over Stanford on the road the week prior, they had little to fear coming east to Chestnut Hill and Alumni Stadium. USC had crushed the Eagles 35–7 a season earlier, and were thought to be a better and deeper team now. BC was a program trying to recapture its past football glory, trying to rebuild itself into a consistent team in the Atlantic Coast Conference, but the Eagles were just two years removed from a two-win season, and they came into the USC game off a 10-point loss to Pittsburgh the week before. They had not beaten a top-10 team in ten years. By the betting line pregame, BC was viewed as a patsy. The Eagles were a 20-point underdog, at home.

But Coach Steve Addazio believed his team had one edge coming into the game—not in speed, strength, or talent, but in emotion. He'd spent the week trying to highlight this game as a great opportunity, not only to beat a top-10 team but to earn a foundational win for a program. He started by giving his players a story to think about.

After two years in his first head-coaching job, at Temple in Philadelphia, Addazio had arrived at BC before the 2013 season and started to build success quickly, lifting the team's record from two wins to seven, and leading the Eagles to a bowl appearance that year. A football lifer who played at Central Connecticut and had tryouts with different pro leagues including the NFL, he became a high school coach close to his alma mater in Cheshire, Connecticut, leading the team to three straight state titles and, at one point, a thirty-four-game winning streak. In 1995, he made the move to college as an assistant coach, with stops at Syracuse, Indiana, and Notre Dame. During his time with the Fighting Irish, he met another assistant, Urban Meyer, who was on his way to his first head-coaching job, at Bowling Green, before going to Utah, and from there to Florida.

Addazio spent six seasons on Meyer's staff in Florida, and was in Gainesville for two national championship teams, in 2006 and 2008. As an assistant, he learned many things from Meyer. Beyond the explosive production and inventiveness of his spread offense, where the field was stretched through the placement and use of the team's fastest athletes, the coaches around Meyer understood another plank of his philosophy: the power of inspiration, a tireless drive to motivate players beyond their own performances and limits. It was an endless passion for Meyer, who was a driven personality bordering on obsessed, always in search of voices, methods, and messages to ratchet up his players' willingness to push themselves, peaking when the ball was kicked off on Saturday. The assistant coaches were expected to carry those messages to their respective position groups through game weeks, and to craft their own. Addazio, a driven and dynamic personality himself, loved the emotional part of the game, tapping into it and mining its force. He created his own messages, and delivered them with fervor.

For Addazio, a huge enemy to team success in a sport as violent and demanding as football was selfishness. One of the many ways he learned to promote the importance of team was in stressing who the team should be playing for: not just themselves or their program but their university. Addazio wanted players to appreciate the ethos of Boston College, its mission, beyond its football goals and standings. He wanted his players to feel a true and deep pride in playing for their school, and to care about its legacy.

"When I was at Florida," Addazio said, "sometimes I used to feel like kids were passing through to get to the [NFL]. I don't want the feeling that you're passing through to get to the league. This is the destination. To me, that's what makes college so great and unique, as opposed to the pros. This is your alma mater. This is a part of you."

To develop that feeling, Addazio installed some new traditions when he arrived. For one, his players were required to learn the words to the college fight song, "For Boston," and after every victory, the team would sing it in the locker room. The coach stressed the importance of the school's motto, "Ever to excel," and he often emphasized the mission of the Jesuit ideal, the core principle the school was founded upon: "Men and Women, for Others."

Addazio found the man around whom he wanted to build a message for the USC game in a BC alumnus, class of 1999. He knew vaguely about Welles Crowther and his death on 9/11 when he arrived on campus in late December 2012. But in the coming months, he found himself compelled by it, and wondered how best to use it, and when.

He found out that some of his players knew the story well, others had a passing familiarity, and some knew nothing about it. The Boston College athletic department, well aware of Welles's time as a varsity lacrosse player, his love for BC, and his actions in the South Tower, had considered how to celebrate his legacy on a broader scale, on the school's biggest competitive stage—at a home football game. USC's visit fit the bill perfectly, a marquee opponent, a date close to the anniversary of September 11, and the game on national television, in prime time. The event was dubbed the first annual Red Bandanna Game, with the hope that it would become a tradition.

Addazio first mentioned the tribute to his players at the start of game week by explaining Crowther's story in very simple terms. At the first team meeting, on Sunday, September 7, he told his team why Welles would be their focus.

"Here's a guy that came here," Addazio said. "He was a guy that kidded around, went to class, worked hard. Loved BC, loved lacrosse, loved his teammates. He was all about service for others, which is what we talk about here. He was an athlete, like them, who did something extraordinary. I just think that kids connected with that.

"We want to be a team, a team that cares for each other. The guy on your right and left is counting on you. We talk about how important the team is. Here's a story about a team guy, a guy that cares more about other people than himself, and lived it, and he was *one of them*. They could taste it, feel it, and touch it. It became real in front of them."

J eff and Alison were thrilled about the tribute game for Welles as soon as BC told them, and excited that it was one of the week's marquee matchups. There would be a lot of attention and a lot of people. Right away, they knew they needed a *lot* of bandannas. With an aggressive campaign using local and social media, the school had encouraged all fans to bring a bandanna of their own to the game. Jeff and Alison's goal was to fill any gap—to have a bandanna for any fans who didn't bring one of their own. They'd given out bandannas before, at many events honoring Welles. This was different. This was a *stadium*.

Working with student groups and officials at BC, they had roughly six thousand ready to be distributed.

A fter his team's walk-through at the stadium, Steve Addazio had them gather in its meeting room. The game plan was already installed. The position groups already understood their assignments. There was only one more element to the preparation.

After talking about Welles's significance all week, Addazio ended by showing the team the ESPN piece about Welles's life, death, and legacy. Many of the players hadn't seen it. The room was silent. When it ended, the room remained that way. Addazio looked at his team and had one thought. *They got it.*

B y the time Jeff and Alison were introduced to the crowd during a break in the game, the scene inside Alumni Stadium was a swaying, waving frenzy of color—not the traditional maroon and gold of the Eagles' uniforms, but red, white, and black. There were bandannas everywhere, many thousands of them throughout the stands. The handkerchiefs were tied around students' heads, flapping in their hands, swirling through the air. The patterns were flashing across the field too, accenting the players' uniforms, striping their helmets, lining their gloves, and marking their cleats. The teardrop designs were stitched into the coaches' sweatshirts and sticking out of their pockets. It wasn't a quaint gesture. This was a powerful homage for the millions tuning in across the country to see.

And then, in the second quarter, the game shifted, not on a mistake by the Trojans, but on a daring strike by the Eagles. Behind 17–13, BC called a gadget play. Quarterback Tyler Murphy took the ball and, with the entire offense rolling right, suddenly flipped a quick pitch to true freshman Sherman Alston, running the opposite way. An end-around reverse. The play worked to perfection. With almost every USC defender following Murphy, the defense tried to shift course back, only to find Alston flying away down the field. Fifty-four yards. Touchdown.

Just like that, BC had the lead. It never again trailed. In every phase of the game, the Eagles rose up. USC ran the ball 29 times for just 20 yards, and gave up 5 sacks. Meanwhile, BC was unstoppable on the ground, running for an astounding 452 yards. Trojan quarterback Cody Kessler threw for 4 touchdowns, kept the Trojans close, but with just three and a half minutes to go, Murphy took the ball, made yet another ball fake, broke beyond the line of scrimmage, and ran 66 yards for the touchdown that sealed the game. USC had never lost to BC. They had now.

Eagles, 37–31.

When the game clock hit zero, students stormed the field, a brigade of bandannas swarming the turf at Alumni Stadium, swallowing the players and coaches. Even the athletic director was seen helping students climb down safely over the walls to join the bedlam. This was the first time an unranked Boston College team had beaten a top-10 opponent since 2002. But the celebration wasn't over.

A football locker room in victory is one of the great spaces in all of sports. Even the musky, sweat-tinged air tastes sweet, as spent players and coaches let themselves go, back inside their cave. The release is pure and giddy, the displays of joy childlike, and often incongruous coming from hulking men sporting bruises and eye black.

As the players took a knee and gathered around the Boston College logo in the center of their locker room late Saturday night, there were still thousands of fans on the stadium field, and hundreds of well-wishers waiting outside the door. The team, thrilled and exhausted, looked up at its head coach, awaiting his message. After Steve Addazio praised the team's toughness and unity, its effort and selflessness, he paused. He wanted to explain what it all meant to one family. Holding a football in his hands, he looked at the young men before him and began to speak again.

"We celebrated this game," Addazio said, "because we celebrated Welles. As a BC man. We celebrated his ability to put other people ahead of himself. Service to others, it's what our university stands for. Someone who had the opportunity to do something for other people, and he paid the ultimate sacrifice to do that."

After acknowledging that he could offer only a symbol of his respect, he turned to his left, looked toward Jeff and Alison, who were standing at the edge of the room, walked over, and presented them with the game ball.

"It was overwhelming," Addazio said, "the emotion in that locker room."

The players stood up and burst into applause, some cheering, many crying. Addazio gave Alison and Jeff the floor.

The players again took a knee as Jeff held the game ball in his arm.

"Just to stand here in front of you," Jeff said, "and look in your faces . . . and see the determination there." His voice was steady. Often it was Alison who shared their son's story, looking out at strangers who'd never known him but wanted to understand. He would cede the floor to her, knowing the emotion would be too great for him. But here, facing a hundred young men, sweaty and proud, he was happy. He was back amid a team, surrounded by athletes, as he had been for so many of Welles's games. These Eagles played a different sport, but wore the same uniform for the same school. He felt connected. He talked about Welles as a peewee football league player, undersized but able to deliver a blow, and the team laughed and smiled. He spoke about Welles's devotion to BC. And he thanked them for their play. "You have honored us greatly."

He put his arm around Alison, standing beside him. She spoke without hesitation.

"The courage and determination you showed, and the teamwork out on the field, was breathtaking," she said. "And we know the odds were against you coming out here. I said, yeah, but they haven't played the game yet."

Jeff had the final word.

"I love these freakin' shoes," he said, pointing down toward the cleats with the red bandanna patterns. The room exploded with laughter. As they made their way out, several players stopped and hugged them. One gave them his game shoes. Another told them he'd chosen BC after learning Welles's story as a high school player in New Jersey.

"I just wanted to tell you how much your son means," he said.

The night held its own meaning for Addazio as he looked back on it, a coach who had endured struggles and success in his career, and who'd reached the pinnacle of the sport.

"This is the highlight," he said, recounting the seven minutes it took for the scene to unfold. "I was more captivated by that than holding the crystal ball after beating Ohio State for the national championship. That moment in that locker room right there, I don't want to take away from our title. But this," he said, and paused. "This was deeper."

After that season, the staff renovated its offices in the football building on campus. Coming off the elevators into the refurbished lobby, the first thing every visitor sees is a wall-long photo from the USC game. It was the only image Addazio considered.

"I wanted the Red Bandanna Game to be on that signature wall," he said. "It just stands for what we want to stand for at BC."

As for the game cleats Jeff received from a player, they sit on a shelf in the house in Upper Nyack on proud display, right next to the game ball.

S*till.*
　　His name has been spoken by the president, his story documented on national television.

His example has been made the foundation of a school curriculum and his number worn on jerseys as a sign of honor.

His identity has been carved in stone on his college campus, and his symbol waved in stadiums, worn by thousands, preserved in a museum, held up to a generation, presented as a standard for living.

Still.

More than a decade after, the absence governs so much of time, an emptiness forever encroaching, a shadow in all light.

Presented with the bandanna, he holds it tightly, squeezing the fabric in his hands.

Were he to open it, spread it, look into its pattern, and let its colors enter and fill him, what would he see there? Would there be a picture or a void? Both or neither? Years later, there would be the relentless fact, too vast to hold inside. He's gone.

"I still weep every day for my son," the father says, his breath seizing. "At some point of every day. Sometimes it's in the morning when I'm shaving. I'm standing in front of the mirror and I have a 19 that is tattooed over my heart. And the memories just keep flooding back. I weep for the loss of a potential that was unfulfilled. What he could have done in his lifetime had he lived

long enough. I weep for the family he never had. I see his contemporaries, his buddies from high school, from college, married, with wonderful little children. I weep for the children that he didn't have.

"But really," Jeff Crowther says, the red bandanna in his hands, his chin high, his gaze firm and strong, "I just weep for the loss of his company."

He stops.

The slide show continues, unbidden and unceasing, the colors of his boy flashing, playing on inside him.

ACKNOWLEDGMENTS

It is no small request to ask a mother and father to share the territory of their lives, at once most precious and most painful, with a stranger. From the first moment I met Jefferson and Alison Crowther, they granted me an extraordinary trust. For this, I owe them far too much to repay or recount. Through dozens of interviews, phone calls, and visits to Upper Nyack, their memories became the living pulse of this narrative. Without them, this book would not be.

Thank you to Welles's sisters, Honor and Paige, for their time, honesty, and insight into Welles, and for traveling back into some of their brightest and hardest memories, to lend a shape to the past. And to the future, as Honor did in naming her first child Welles Remy Fagan, born in 2004.

As a portrait of strength and a proof of spirit, the Crowthers are as much a wonder as they are a family.

For information on the Welles Remy Crowther Trust, please visit www .crowthertrust.org. To learn about the educational and leadership curricula based on Welles's story, please visit www.redbandannaproject.org.

The idea for a fuller narrative of Welles's life came not from me, but from Scott Moyers at Penguin Press, who first saw its possibilities. He has worn every hat and played every role necessary in this book's creation. His endless patience, constant encouragement, and sure-handed editing have been as essential as air. Through the doubts, thanks for being mine in the struggle.

Also at Penguin Press, I am grateful for the contributions of the open-hearted Christopher Richards, for his careful and empathetic reading of the manuscript; Claire Vaccaro, for her strong and clear design; Darren Haggar, for creating so many versions of the evocative bandanna jacket; Sarah Hutson and Tessa Meischeid, house publicists who embraced this story before the pages were close to complete; Matt Boyd, the marketing maestro and an author's favorite voice of introduction; and Ann Godoff, who saw the good in this story, and encouraged its place in the world.

David Black, literary agent and one of the toughest men I know, endured more than I can imagine in the time between receiving this book's proposal and its first manuscript, and always found time for support, counsel, and straight talk.

Thanks as well to Nick Khan at CAA, a consigliere more than an agent, whose interest and guidance from the book's commission to its completion were selfless and unflagging.

One of the first suggestions I received in the process was to enlist a good researcher. Here, I exceeded all advice by gaining the help of my colleague at ESPN William Weinbaum. To overstate Willie's contributions would be impossible, and to consider his work as research only would be entirely wrong. The best reporter I know, he served as the book's conscience and shepherd, its eyes and heart. The pages bear his imprint as much as mine.

I am grateful for those involved in the ESPN feature on Welles, without whose work this book would not have been written; Drew Gallagher, whose passion for the story came long before my own, and whose producing of the television piece remains a lesson to me in my work; Gregg Hoerdemann and his crew, who captured the indelible images that brought Welles's journey to life; Tim Horgan at Bluefoot, for his singular editing talent; and Victor Vitarelli, who oversaw the project and helped it reach its best form.

Also at ESPN, my gratitude goes to John Skipper and John Wildhack, for allowing me to pursue this story in a different venue.

Thanks, too, to all those who helped me at Sandler O'Neill, the firm that refused to fall. Over the past five years, Jimmy Dunne has been open and available at every turn. And to those employed there, then and still, who shared their memories of Welles and the stories of their survival, I am grateful.

To my brother, Robert, who worked for more than a decade on the eighty-first floor of the South Tower of the World Trade Center, and who left his office there in the spring of 2001, I am grateful. To my sister, Doretta, whose meeting across the street from the towers on September 11 was canceled early that morning, I am grateful for you, too.

I wrote the majority of this book in the house my father, Ralph, built. I did most of the written work at his old desk. I'd like to believe his spirit has read these pages. I am beholden to him, forever.

My mother, Eileen, was my first and most faithful reader of the words written in that house nearly every day. Her encouragement and empathy, her patience and cheer were boundless and made a greater difference than I can ever describe. Thank you, Mom.

To our son, Jack, and our daughter, Tessa, you are the joyous purpose of all.

To Dianne, to whom this book is dedicated: The door opens . . .

How will I do this?

You are how. And will be, always.

A NOTE ON SOURCES

From the original telling of Welles's story as a television feature in 2011 through the completion of this narrative five years later, I am deeply indebted to many—for their time and memory, their work and care, their knowledge and patience, for their help in the reporting of this book.

I am grateful to the following for the interviews they granted and, in them, the insights and information they shared: Steve Addazio, Jessica Alberti, Marcie Baeza-Sauer, Michael Barch, Lee Burns, Matt Casamassima, Peter Cassano, Salvatore Cassano, Paige Crowther Charbonneau, Alison Crowther, Jefferson Crowther, Timothy Curry, James Devery, Matt Dickey, Matt Drowne, Scott Dunn, Jimmy Dunne, Tim Epstein, Honor Crowther Fagan, Chris Ferrarone, John Finlay, Karen Fishman, Mark Fitzgibbon, Drew Gallagher, James Gilroy, David Gottlieb, Jon Hess, Willie Hopkins, Johnny Howells, Lee Ielpi, Tyler Jewell, Mary Jos, Stephen Joseph, Matt Katchmar, John Kline, Jane Lerner, George Leuchs, Rob Lewis, Susie DeFrancis Lind, Angelo Mangia, Ben Marra, Pat McCavanagh, Natalie McIver, Dave Moreno, Ed Moy, Charles Murphy, Edward Nicholls, Keith O'Brien, Matthew O'Keefe, Justin Patnode, Nyack historian Win Perry, Chuck Platz, Jessica Quintana Hess, Karim Raoul, Chris Reynolds, Matt Rosen, John Ryan, John Scott, Jonathan Sperman, Jody Steinglass, Tom Sullivan, Gerry Sussman, Kevin Tiernan, James Tremble, Chris Varmon, Paul Wanamaker, Scott Wiener, and Ling Young.

Most of the interviews were transcribed and archived by NoNotes.com.

While the vast majority of this book comes from primary source material gained through interviews with those listed above, the reader surely understands the depth of reporting done on the September 11 attacks, across myriad outlets by hundreds, if not thousands, of journalists. Of those works, I leaned most heavily on several.

As mentioned in the text, *102 Minutes,* by Jim Dwyer and Kevin Flynn, was invaluable, not only in helping to convey the context around Welles's experience that day, but also in ways broader and more fundamental. The history of the towers, the intricacies of their design, the accounts of the survivors, and the painstaking chronology of those minutes between the first plane's strike and the second tower's fall are essential to any understanding of the day's events, and of Welles's movements that morning.

Also noted in the text, "Fighting to Live as the Towers Died" the *Times'* piece reported by Dwyer, Flynn, Eric Lipton, James Glanz, and Ford Fessenden, was the first mention of Welles, without name, as the man with the red handkerchief helping others on the seventy-eighth floor. In addition, the *Times'* accompanying piece, "Accounts from the South Tower," included vital interviews that aided in telling this story. In particular, Lipton's interview with Judy Wein and Fessenden's interview with Ling Young were essential in adding to the primary interviews done for this project.

A book that was especially important in helping to understand the challenges and dimension of the fallen towers, and the pile's unique horror, was William Langewiesche's singular *American Ground: Unbuilding the World Trade Center.* His chronicle of the recovery effort and the pile's clearing deeply informed this account.

For the plainest facts rooted in the attacks, most involving exact timings and numerical totals, I relied on *The Complete 9/11 Commission Report (The National Commission on Terrorist Attacks upon the United States)* as a definitive source.

The Press Office of the Fire Department of New York provided information, as did the New York City Fire Museum, about the FDNY and its posthumous honoring of Welles as a firefighter. And the Social Security Administration is the source for the data on newborns named Welles.

Terry Szuplat, the White House speechwriter who worked with President Obama on his remarks for the dedication of the 9/11 Memorial Museum, given May 15, 2014, responded to our questions about the context and contents of the speech.

The Boston College athletic department was generous in its help and was an invaluable resource.

Welles's story was chronicled, in dozens of ways, long before I first learned of his valor. As mentioned in the text, Jane Lerner was the first to report his identity, as the man in the red bandanna, in her work for *The Journal News,* and played a key role in the nation's discovery of his actions.

I also owe a debt to the following journalists and their respective works, for the reporting that helped to provide greater context and important information on other subjects that played a role in Welles's story. In each case, the pieces were deeply helpful in the insights provided, during the research and writing of this book:

"For Many on 9/11, Survival Was No Accident," *USA Today,* 12/20/2001, Dennis Cauchon.

"Requiems for Victims: A Time for Prayer and Reflection," *The Journal News,* 9/30/2001, Nancy Cacioppo.

"Volunteer Firefighter Found at Ground Zero Laid to Rest," *The Journal News,* 3/31/2002, Jane Lerner.

"Sandler O'Neill's Journey from Ground Zero," *Fortune,* 9/1/2011, David Whitford.

Portraits of 9/11/01, "The Collected Portraits of Grief from the *New York Times,*" Times Books, New York Times staff.

"Nyack Sketch Log: 150 Years of Volunteer Firefighting," *Nyack News & Views,* 8/27/2013, Bill Batson.

"After September 11: Starting Over," *Fortune,* 1/21/2002, updated 9/11/2015, Katrina Booker.

"Her Heroes," CBS News, 9/4/2002, Tatiana Morales.

"Upper Nyack Dedicates Plaque to Harry Wanamaker Jr.," *Nyack-Piermont Patch,* 6/10/2012, Adam Littman.

"A Close Bond and the Unending Toll of 9/11," *The New York Times,* 6/8/2012, David Dunlap.

"Fatally Stabbed Nyack Man Remembered as Teammate, Served Time for Assault," Patch.com, 6/27/2011, Kevin Zawacki.

"A Man of the Land, Ozzie Fischer Jr. Dies on Island He Nurtured for Nine Decades," *Vineyard Gazette,* 7/28/2011, Julia Wells.

"Hudson River Rescue Still Defines Upgrade of Fire Dept.'s Marine Unit," *The New York Times,* 1/14/2011, Liz Robbins.

"Boston College Uses Emotion and Its Running Game to Shock No. 9 USC," SI.com, 9/14/2014, Pete Thamel.

"Bosley Crowther, 27 Years a Critic of Films for *Times,* Is Dead at 75," *The New York Times,* 3/8/1981, Robert D. McFadden.

"Red Bandanna Honoring 9-11 Hero Goes Perfectly with UCF School Colors," *Orlando Sentinel,* 9/6/2011, Mike Bianchi.

"A Year of Living Gratefully," *Golf Digest,* 12/2002, Bill Fields and Tim Rosaforte.

"After 5 Years, His Voice Can Still Crack," *The New York Times,* 9/9/2006, Joe Nocera.

"Obama Honors Victims of Bin Laden at Ground Zero," *The New York Times,* 5/5/2011, Mark Landler.

"Postcard from NY: Iconic Images," *Nyack News & Views,* 6/24/2012, Alison Perry.

"If You're Thinking of Living in: Nyack," *The New York Times,* 8/14/1988, Jenny Lyn Bader.

Marine1fdny.com, website of *Marine 1.*

"The Long Good-Bye," *New York* magazine, Robert Kolker.

"Toni Morrison's Manuscripts Spared in Christmas Fire," *The New York Times,* 12/28/1993, Robert D. McFadden.

"The Heart of a Firefighter: 9/11 Hero Welles Crowther Named Honorary Firefighter," *FDNY News,* 12/2006.

America Remembers, CNN special reports, 2002.